James Cary is a sitcom writer 1
Miranda, Bluestone 42, Thank
Hut 33. He's also a member of ... General Synod and the
Archbishops' Council. He blogs on religion and comedy and
co-presents podcasts *Sitcom Geeks* and *Cooper and Cary Have
Words*. He is the author of *The Sacred Art of Joking*, a look at
how religion and comedy intersect (SPCK, 2018).

THE GOSPEL ACCORDING TO A SITCOM WRITER

James Cary

First published in Great Britain in 2021

Society for Promoting Christian Knowledge
36 Causton Street
London SW1P 4ST
www.spck.org.uk

British Library Cataloguing-in-Publication Data
A catalogue record for this book is available from the British Library

ISBN 978–0–281–08563–7
eBook ISBN 978–0–281–08599–6

Typeset by Falcon Oast Graphic Art Ltd
First printed in Great Britain by Jellyfish Print Solutions
Subsequently digitally printed in Great Britain

eBook by Falcon Oast Graphic Art Ltd

Produced on paper from sustainable forests

Contents

Introduction

What sort of book is *The Gospel According to a Sitcom Writer*?

This book is funny. But it is also Christian. These tend not to go together.

When a bookshop gets a whiff of Christianity, it puts it in the 'Religion' section. You know where it is, right? Through the coffee shop, up the back stairs by the wrapping paper and board games, past the loos (one is out of order, sorry), keep going until you come to Ordnance Survey Maps, then past Personal Finance, down a couple more steps (mind the low ceiling) and there, you'll find a few dozen books on religion.

Somehow, religion, the single greatest motivator throughout human history and across much of the world today, is deemed 'niche'. What a time to be alive.[1][2] If you are wondering what sort of book this is, allow me to explain.

The sitcom bit

I am a sitcom writer. My first sitcom, *Think the Unthinkable*, was broadcast on Radio 4 on 16 October 2001[3] and I've been

---

1 You'd think this book section would be like an oasis on a hot day for religious people. But the Religion section in a bookshop normally contains books religious people don't actually read. If you are religious and well informed, your tastes tend to be more specific and granular, thus the religious section in a big bookshop is normally a disappointment.

2 Yes, this is going to be one of those books with footnotes – but at the bottom of the page so you actually read them. Not at the back which you never refer to and are there to point people to other books that the author has read so that you don't have to.

3 I don't want to show off, but that first episode won a Silver at the Sony Radio

fairly busy ever since. Sitcom writing is an unusual way to make a living. The pay is irregular and lumpy. You put in hours of work on a new show for zero reward. And then you get a couple of hundred pounds because your episode of *My Family* has been available to view on BA flights for the past 18 months. The amount of work you do often bears little relation to the money paid. TV pays five times more than radio, even though the audience figures might be the same, or even favour radio. The life of a writer, even a moderately successful sitcom writer, is uncertain.

So why put myself through the uncertainty and the trauma of having to make a roomful of three hundred complete strangers laugh three times a minute for half an hour, with the results broadcast on national TV or radio? It's a very good question. I'm glad I asked it.

Essentially, it comes down to this: why do I want to make people laugh? For some it's a defence mechanism, perhaps to prevent bullying at school, or a form of emotional self-protection. For others, it's a need to be wanted and loved. The roar of the crowd can be intoxicating. Many stand-up comedians would admit to being addicted to it. I don't think any of those are my main motivation.

I have occasionally been responsible for audiences laughing loud, long and hard. The laughter you hear on the TV and the radio isn't fake. The audience is normally real. I've sat in audiences for dozens of recordings of episodes of *Think the Unthinkable*, *Hut 33*, *My Hero* or umpteen radio shows I've written with Milton Jones. The people around me have no idea that the writer is sitting next to them. I don't need them

---

Awards in the comedy category, only losing out to *I'm Sorry I Haven't A Clue*. It meant I got to sit next to Barry Cryer all evening, which was hilarious.

to know I am one of the writers. In fact, I much prefer the anonymity. This could make my desire to hear that laughter more puzzling. But actually, it makes sense of it.

So I'm not a sitcom writer because I find that sound of laughter addictive. I find it essential. If I hear the laugh, I know the joke has worked. And if I don't hear the laugh, I know the joke hasn't worked. It's pretty basic, and one of the reasons I don't really want to write drama – how do you know if it's working?

For me, writing comedy is an endless, fascinating puzzle. Coming up with a joke for each character in each situation is like solving a cryptic crossword clue. Each clue has multiple ingredients that need to be accounted for, and you know the right answer because it fits with 3 Down and has the correct number of letters. For me, that sound of the laugh means I've found the answer. I've cracked the puzzle. I've found a way to make that character in that scene in that story say something that's objectively funny. And it feels good. When that happens, to quote Eric Liddell, 'I feel God's pleasure.' That's because I don't see my job as a way to earn money and satisfy my curiosity. It is a divine calling.

The gospel bit

I care what God thinks about the comedy that I write, since I'm a Christian. I'm not a 'small c' cultural Christian. I'm a big C, all-in, confessing Christian. Over the years, I've been involved in Christian conferences, conventions and festivals and the opportunity has arisen for me to perform, and I've done so with some success. I define success as the audience mostly laughing in the places I had expected and planned.

Given the circumstances of these performances, I've been playing to biblically literate audiences who have a pretty good idea of what the Bible says and how it sounds. Being a word-smith, and an amateur theologian, I've tried to make the most of these opportunities to create comedy that speaks directly into the Christian experience.

Many have found this refreshing and surprising. Not many people do this sort of thing, and you certainly won't find any-thing like it in the mainstream media these days. The size and location of the Religion section in a three-storey bookshop is one manifestation of our society's failure to understand religion generally and Christianity particularly.[4] Moreover, Christians are very poorly represented on TV, and you'll see a chapter on that very subject, along with a few reasons for it, and a bit of a rant, which you might find cathartic.

This project has also given me numerous comedy puzzles to solve that are even more complex than writing an episode of *My Family* for BBC1. How can I be funny in a way that takes the Bible seriously, does not belittle Jesus Christ and laughs at our own petty vanities and foibles while being enlightening and increasing our understanding? And how can I heighten the comedy already present in Scripture?

This book is a result of those comic explorations. In the pages that follow, you will find a mix of writing, much of

---

4 During various COVID-19 lockdowns in 2020, the government never really understood that religion was more than a private matter, or prefer-ence. Opening churches for prayer during the week was not really what millions of Anglicans, Catholics, Charismatics and other denominations wanted. Whether you believe that church is about the sacrament or collec-tive listening to the preaching of the Word, you need to turn up in person. It's incarnational. Our profoundly secular government did not really understand this.

4

which plays around with biblical texts in ways that I hope readers find playful and illuminating rather than irreverent or idiotic.

It is all, of course, open to debate and even wilful misunderstanding. Christians are brilliant at the latter, as I explored in my previous book, *The Sacred Art of Joking*,[5] in which I explain how comedy works and how it goes wrong, especially in the realm of religion. All too often, Christian leaders find themselves following in the footsteps of the Pharisees and Sadducees, and finding themselves to be holier than Jesus. But you can read more about that there.[6]

No justification

In this book I try to let the material mostly speak for itself. There is much truth to the title of theologian Hans Rookmaaker's book, *Art Needs No Justification*.[7] But there is also truth in what mums say to children: 'Stop showing off.' Is this art, heresy or showing off? You be the judge.

Much quasi-biblical material in this book is presented with words along the lines of, 'Early manuscripts do not include the following', which reflects the fact that some parts of the Gospel accounts are not considered to be original, canonical or authoritative. This strikes me as a helpful caveat for my writings, which are clearly not canonical, have no authority and aren't wholly original. Surely Christians through the

---

5 Published by SPCK, 2019.
6 *The Sacred Art of Joking* is available in some good bookshops, probably in the Religion section, so don't get your hopes up.
7 H. R. Rookmaaker, *Art Needs No Justification* (Leicester: InterVarsity Press, 1978).

centuries must have had these thoughts before me? Maybe it takes someone with the chutzpah of a sitcom writer to actually write them down and show other people. Either way, I present to you *The Gospel According to a Sitcom Writer*. Run opening titles.

৫৪৪০

The Ascension

Let us begin at the end, with the Ascension of Jesus. Luke records this at the end of his Gospel and again at the beginning of Acts.[1] The Christian church names a Sunday after it so it must be quite important. But have you considered how odd it is that Jesus ascends into heaven? And don't you think the disciples at the time would have thought so? Sometimes, the Gospels record the reactions of the disciples to extraordinary events, but not here. So my version does. We begin at the end of the Gospel According to Matthew.[2]

But the eleven disciples went into Galilee, to the mountain where Jesus had sent them. When they saw him, they bowed down to him; but some doubted. Jesus came to them and spoke to them, saying, 'All authority has been given to me in heaven and on earth. Go and make disciples of all nations, baptizing them in the name of the Father and of the Son and of the Holy Spirit, teaching them to observe all things that I commanded you. Behold, I am with you always, even to the end of the age.'[3]

---

1 It is also in the contested final verses of Mark's Gospel, labelled, 'Earlier manuscripts do not include . . .', so this is probably the perfect way to start this book.

2 Throughout the book, I don't use the traditional 'St' title as I'm one of those Reformed types who would argue that the New Testament always applies the title 'saint' to all believers.

3 In case you were wondering, the version being used (and abused) in this book is the *World English Bible*. You probably haven't heard of it, but I've chosen it because it's fairly literal (important) and, crucially, is free from copyright, which removes legal complications about changing scriptural

Early manuscripts do not include the following

After saying this, he was taken up into a cloud while they were watching, and they could no longer see him.

And Peter said, 'Well, that was weird.'

And the disciples agreed. It was weird.

But John said, 'Did not our Lord say, "I am ascending to my Father and your Father"?'

And Peter said, 'Did he?'

And John said, 'Yes. He did. And it's going into my book.'

'Wow,' said Peter. 'Jesus has been gone ten seconds and you're already thinking about book deals.'

And John said, 'I will write it so anyone who reads it may believe that Jesus is the Christ, the Son of God, and that by believing they may have life in his name.'

And Peter said, 'Urgh, well, if you put it like that, I suppose it's fine.'

And the disciples remained on the Mount of Olives, singing hymns and praising God.

Then Thomas said, 'I doubted, but now I believe.'

And Peter said, 'Yes. You doubted. And now you believe.'

Thomas said, 'Do you think anyone will, you know, remember that "incident"?'

'"Incident"?' said Peter.

'You know,' said Thomas, 'in the locked room?'

'No,' said the disciples. 'Hardly at all. Completely understandable. Jesus came back. You weren't there. You didn't believe us. Fingers in wounds. Perfectly natural.'

---

texts and translations, causing confusion or breaches of copyright terms and conditions. It's just easier this way. Okay, no more footnotes. Sorry.

'Oh, good,' said Thomas with great relief. 'I'd hate for three years of exemplary service as a disciple and a possible future as an apostle to be completely ruined for ever because of one week-long crisis of faith.'

'Forget about it,' said James. 'It's not going to happen.'

Then John spoke. 'That said, it does provide a useful set-piece scene that helps with the overall resurrection narrative. It certainly adds credibility to the account.'

'Oh, great,' said Thomas.

'I haven't decided whether to use it or not,' said John.

'If you stitch me up,' said Thomas, 'and I'm referred to as unbelieving Thomas, or faithless Thomas . . .'

'What about doubting Thomas?' said James.

'Ooh, that's good,' said John. 'Not that I'm definitely using that in my book. Everything's very much up for grabs.'

'Why am I the doubting one?' said Thomas. 'Peter denied Jesus three times to a little girl.'

'She wasn't that little,' said Peter.

'Should have kept your head down,' came a voice from the back.

'And you are?' asked Peter.

'Bartholomew,' said Bartholomew.

'Bartholomew?' said Peter.

'Bartholomew!' said Bartholomew. 'I'm a disciple.'

'Are you?'

'Yeah. In Mark. Look it up. I just don't say much.'

'Nor me,' said Thaddeus.

'Argh!' said Peter. 'Where did you come from?'

'Don't say anything and people will think you're clever,' said Thaddeus. 'That's my motto.'

Thomas wept.

'Chin up,' said Peter. 'Did not our Lord himself say, "There's no such thing as bad publicity"?'

'No!' said Thomas.

'Well, remember the parable that Jesus told,' said Peter. 'How does it go? Ah yes, a king went on a long journey and he left three men to work in his vineyard. Or was it a winepress? That's it, the son fell in the wine-press. No, that's not right. Hang on. Bear with.'

'Ooh! I've got one,' said Bartholomew. 'A Pharisee, a priest and a Samaritan walk into a bar . . .'

'You see? This is why you should keep your mouth shut!' said Thaddeus.

'This isn't helping!' said Thomas.

Two men dressed in white stood beside them. They didn't like to interrupt. One said to the other, 'Jesus wants them to make disciples of all nations? Good luck with that.' They walked away, shaking their heads.

This is not the word of the Lord.
Thanks be to God.

☙❧

We will return to the Ascension and what happened next later in the book. For now, let us go back to the beginning.

The first joke in John's Gospel

I have a lot of sympathy with Nathanael. He's a disciple of Jesus only mentioned in John's Gospel. Many Bible scholars believe that Nathanael was also known as Bartholomew, but maybe he went into obscurity precisely because he attempted a joke early in the Gospel.

The joke passes by so quickly, most people miss it. It's understandable. Few people are expecting to find jokes in John's Gospel. At first glance, it doesn't promise many laughs. The 'In the beginning' beginning makes it feel very austere, but once you get into the meat of the Gospel, especially the first 11 chapters, you find quite a lot of comic incidents.

So let's take a closer look at some material that may have been cut from the early versions of John's Gospel to see why Nathanael is not the household name he might have been.

On the next day, [Jesus] was determined to go out into Galilee, and he found Philip. Jesus said to him, 'Follow me.' Now Philip was from Bethsaida, of the city of Andrew and Peter. Philip found Nathanael, and said to him, 'We have found him, of whom Moses in the law, and the prophets, wrote: Jesus of Nazareth, the son of Joseph.'

Nathanael said to him, 'Can any good thing come out of Nazareth?'

Early manuscripts do not include the following
Philip said to him, 'What's that supposed to mean?'

'Well, Nazareth?' said Nathanael. 'This messianic figure comes from Nazareth? I don't think so.'

Philip said to him, 'What's wrong with Nazareth?'

Nathanael said to him, 'What's right with Nazareth? Am I right?'

Nathanael raised a hand for Philip to high-five. But Philip high-fived him not.

'Don't leave me hanging,' said Nathanael.

'I'm not seeing it. Seriously, Nate. What is wrong with Nazareth?'

'Oh, don't be like this,' said Nathanael. 'It's just a joke. Honestly, you can't say anything these days.'

'Is this the place for jokes? I really don't think so. Especially about the people of Nazareth. During a time of political unrest? These stereotypes just aren't helpful. You wanna have a long, hard look at yourself, Nate.'

'You wanna do this?' said Nathanael. 'Fine. Answer me this. What happened in Nazareth hundreds of years ago which gives the place huge historical significance in the history of our people?'

'What?'

'NOTHING! That's what!' said Nathanael. 'No thing. It's a backwater. A no place. A new town. It's the Milton Keynes of Israel.'

'What's Milton Keynes?'

'I don't know. That must have been prophetic,' said Nathanael. 'Hey, maybe I'm a prophet. The beard needs work, but I'm getting the hang of the wild-eyed stare.'

'Nate. You're not a prophet. You're just a bloke who's

prejudiced about people from Nazare— Hey, wait a minute. You're from the town next door, aren't you? Cana?'

There was a long pause. Nathanael looked away.

'I might be,' said Nathanael.

'Daaah!' said Philip. 'Pathetic local rivalry. You can't bear the thought of your neighbour being home to the Lamb of God who takes away the sin of the world.'

'You what?' said Nathanael. 'What does that mean?'

'No idea. Looks like I'm prophetic too.'

Philip raised a hand for Nathanael to high-five. And Nathanael did not high-five him.

'Look,' said Nathanael, 'all I'm saying is that everything happens for a reason.'

'Okay, you are definitely not a prophet. That's just faux folk philosophy.'

'I'm talking about the sovereignty of God, and putting it in layman's terms! I'm a man of the people,' said Nathanael.

Philip looked around.

'I tell you one thing that's for sure,' said Philip. 'You know where the Messiah won't be from? Samaria.'

'Ha!' Nathanael laughed. 'Yeah, Samaritans are the WORST.'

Philip raised a hand for Nathanael to high-five. And Nathanael did high-five him.

Then . . . Philip said to him, 'Come and see.'

And they went. And saw.

This is not the word of the Lord.
Thanks be to God.

ೞ ೲ

The wedding thank-you note

S oon after Nathanael's attempt at a joke, Jesus and a few friends are invited to a wedding. Jesus is lucky to have been invited. John records, 'The third day, there was a wedding in Cana of Galilee. Jesus' mother was there. Jesus also was invited . . .' Not sure the Supreme Being has ever been referred to as a 'plus one' before, but there we go. Thanks to the plus one, Jesus manufactures one of his most momentous and memorable miracles. (Try saying that after several gallons of wine.)

Apart from Jesus turning water into wine, one of the oddest things about this account is so obvious, no one ever notices it: who were the happy couple? We have no idea. Poor Steve and Becky. Their wedding was the backdrop to this miracle, and they never got a mention. Perhaps they complained. But how would they do that?

This puts me in mind of the agony aunt in *The Spectator* magazine. On this page, passive-aggressive members of the upper middle class write to Mary to explain how awful and tiresome their friends are, and to ask how to be free from their embarrassing vanity or boorishness. Mary is quite the expert at dealing with these letters. She is forever explaining how an ungrateful godson can be tricked into saying 'thank you' for an expensive eighteenth birthday present even though the givers protest that 'we don't want to be thanked, honestly, but we do feel it's important that he learns the lesson of gratitude'. Yeah, right.

So maybe the happy couple from the world's most famous wedding wrote to an agony aunt, Lydia, to explain their own dilemma.

Dear Lydia,

My husband and I just got back from our honeymoon (two weeks on the coast in Tyre – BLISS!) and have become aware that our wedding is being written up for some publication we've never heard of. We think the 'leak' is from a lady called Mary, an old friend from Nazareth who, frankly, we've always felt a bit sorry for. (Not only is she from Nazareth but she was also pregnant before marriage and gave birth in a stable! Can you IMAGINE?) She brought her rather odd eldest son, Jesus, who brought some chums. It seemed a little cheeky but we didn't want to say anything. But to cap it all, one of Jesus' entourage appeared to be taking notes! How can we find out what he's planning to do with his account without embarrassing poor Mary?

We are worried this would-be society hack might mention us by name, saying we had run out of wine, which would, of course, be incredibly embarrassing. But we hadn't. It turns out we had over-ordered and saved the best until last. Who knew?

But that's not the worst of it. After everyone had enjoyed this excellent wine, there was a fair amount of confusion and 'hijinks' and many of the presents were separated from their tags. What do we do? We have no idea if the toasting forks were all from the same person or nine different people. (Why do newly-weds get so many toasting forks?!) Please help!

Eternally yours,
Rebekah

Lydia writes

Dear Rebekah,

What an awkward situation. I hope this son of Mary isn't going to make a habit of causing a scene. My advice is to write to Mary and ask her to check that her son's friend is going to spell your name correctly. Say you're a 'Rebekah', not a 'Rebecca', 'Becky' or, heaven forfend, 'Bex'. (Eurgh!) Ask where you can see the account in print, saying you're worried about the reputation of the caterers, who were marvellous despite some ugly rumours about the wine. Maybe Jesus and his gatecrashing friends are to blame for the shortage.

Since this unofficial scribe was taking such detailed notes, you could ask him if he made a note of who gave what present. Might as well make the most of this impertinent fellow's snooping at your wedding!

But don't worry. If Mary's son is a bit eccentric, he shouldn't attract too much attention in the long run. The gawpers will move on. This wedding report probably won't appear in a publication that many people will actually read.

Best of luck with it!

Lydia

 C3 80

Wot, no parables?

Or: Why John's Gospel is so different from the others

The most famous wedding outside the Bible took place in 1981. Approximately 28.4 million people in the UK watched Prince Charles marry Lady Diana Spencer. Hundreds of millions watched globally.

A few months later, a fictional wedding drew an audience of 17.8 million viewers in the UK. On BBC1, Audrey fforbes-Hamilton (Penelope Keith) married Richard de Vere (Peter Bowles) in the finale of the smash-hit sitcom, *To the Manor Born*. The audience figures seem large when you look back, but there are two crucial factors people often miss.

The first is that, in 1981, if you wanted to change channel, you had to get off the sofa or despatch a child (usually the youngest, i.e. me). The TV remote control was still the stuff of science fiction. The second factor to remember is that there were only three channels.

But then, on 2 November 1982, Channel 4 began. And it seemed very different from the other three. A bit like John's Gospel. But we'll come to back that.

My love of sitcom

On its very first night, Channel 4 showed *The Comic Strip Presents . . . Five Go Mad in Dorset*, starring all the cool kids in comedy like French and Saunders, Adrian Edmondson and Robbie Coltrane. At first, Channel 4 didn't have much success with homegrown sitcoms (e.g. *Chelmsford 123*), not least because it could import them from America. Therefore, I spent many happy hours of my life watching *Roseanne* and *The Cosby Show*, before graduating to *Cheers*, and *M*A*S*H* on BBC2, when I was allowed to stay up late enough. From an early age, I associated sitcom with smart speech and American accents. I was hooked. It set me on a path of wanting to emulate these shows.

Sadly, by the time I was writing TV sitcoms, I was working in a world with multi-channel, remote-controlled TVs in the age of Freeview and Sky TV. Audience figures reflected this fragmentation. This was made especially obvious when the episode of BBC1 mainstream mainstay, *My Family*, that I wrote was broadcast on 28 May 2004. It drew 4.4 million viewers. In my defence, it was up against the last ever episode of *Friends* on Channel 4, so I don't take it too personally.

Back to the Gospel

I didn't mind losing to Channel 4 that night. It was home to a childhood favourite, *Sesame Street*, which had just enough Muppets to keep it interesting. One regular feature from that show sticks in my mind and is relevant to our return to John's Gospel. They would split the screen in four and show three kids doing something like bouncing a ball. In one section was another kid doing something else, like playing with a hula hoop. A catchy song played in which we were told that 'Three of these kids belong together, three of these kids are kind of the same. But one of these kids is doing his own thing . . .'

In the New Testament, the kid who's doing his own thing is John, the Gospel writer. You have the Synoptic Gospel writers, Matthew, Mark and Luke, who 'belong together' all merrily bouncing a ball. They overlap, use similar sources and consistently cover the same events, albeit from slightly different angles.

But John is out there hula-hooping, doing his own thing. Only in John's Gospel does Jesus raise Lazarus from the dead, meet Nicodemus and the woman at the well, and wash the disciples' feet. And don't go looking for any exorcisms, transfigurations, ascensions, temptations in the wilderness or calls to repentance. In today's parlance, you'd call John a reboot.

Wot, no parables?[1]

Another astonishing omission from John's Gospel is parables. Parables there are none. No fictional Samaritans, prodigal sons tending pigs, or seeds falling on stony ground. Jesus makes heavy use of metaphors and allusion, and the I AM statements are essential. But there are no short stories that begin with, 'A man went out early in the morning to hire labourers for his vineyard,' or, 'A man about to go on a journey summoned his stewards'. None of those. But it's okay. I've written some.

And so I present The Parable of the Lost Key. You will

---

1   If you're 45 or older, you may remember an advertising campaign, 'Wot, no meat?' If you're much older, you may remember Mr Chad, a cartoon figure of graffiti, commenting on shortages during rationing – e.g. 'Wot, no sugar?'

notice that it is Peter telling the parable and not Jesus. A red line for me is having Jesus say things he did not say.[2]

I'm also drawn to Peter, who seems to channel the spirit of Homer Simpson in the Gospel accounts. Perhaps when the twelve or the seventy were sent out by Jesus (neither of which occur in John's Gospel), Peter would plausibly try to retell or expand some of Jesus' parables, but get it wrong in the process. You can read the results for yourself:

Early manuscripts do not include the following

Now the tax collectors and 'sinners' were all gathering round Peter, but the Pharisees and teachers of the law muttered, 'This man welcomes sinners and eats with them.' Then Peter told them this parable.

'Suppose one of you has a hundred keys and loses one. Does he not leave the 99 keys, shout loudly and say, "Where on earth did I put that key?"?

'Will his wife not say to him, "Where did you last have it?"?

'And will he not reply, "If I knew that I wouldn't have lost it, would I?"?

'And will she not say, "I was only trying to be helpful"?

'And will he not say, "I know, I know. I'm sorry. It's just this always happens"?

'And will she not say, "Well, if you put them on that hook like I'm always telling you, then maybe . . . "?

---

2 I realize this is theologically problematic, as I believe Paul's words in 2 Timothy 3.16 that 'Every Scripture is God-breathed', and therefore Jesus' words as presented in the Bible aren't technically any more or less authoritative than all the other words. For me, it's all or nothing. In fact, for me, it's all. Not nothing.

'And will he not recall the proverbs of Solomon, which describe a nagging wife being like a leaking roof? And will he dare to say this?

'And will she not remind him that there is a dripping tap that needs fixing that he said he'd get round to last weekend but hasn't?

'Then at last he finds the key in his other trousers.

'Then he will call his friends and neighbours together, saying, "Rejoice with me; I found my lost key."

'And they will think he is a bit odd because it is only a key and hardly something worth gathering your friends and neighbours for, and they will shuffle out embarrassed and slightly afraid.

'Truly, truly I say to you,'[3] said Peter, 'there will be more rejoicing over one lost key that has been found than there will ever be over a lost coin.'

And everyone looked at Peter.

'Teacher,' said one of the disciples, 'where exactly is this going?'

And Peter replied, 'Do you still not understand?'

And they said, 'Do you?'

And he said, 'No.'

This is not the word of the Lord.
Thanks be to God.

ର ଡ

---

3 I put 'Truly, truly I say to you' to make it more John-like where Jesus uses that expression a lot.

That escalated quickly

> Boy, that escalated quickly. I mean, that really got out of hand fast.
>
> *Anchorman*[1]

This memorable line from Ron Burgundy (Will Ferrell) in *Anchorman* has become a modern-day meme. In the film, there is a fight between rival news teams which gets very nasty and comically violent, leading Ron Burgundy to reflect afterwards, 'Boy, that escalated quickly. I mean, that really got out of hand fast.'

In John 2, we see Jesus cleansing the temple, leading to a comic moment of serious escalation. It is an unlikely place for comedy. Have a look at John 2.13–16 (which I have not tinkered with):

The Passover of the Jews was at hand, and Jesus went up to Jerusalem. He found in the temple those who sold oxen, sheep, and doves, and the changers of money sitting. He made a whip of cords, and threw all out of the temple, both the sheep and the oxen; and he poured out the changers' money and overthrew their tables. To those who sold the doves, he said, 'Take these things out of here! Don't make my Father's house a marketplace!'

---

1 *Anchorman: The legend of Ron Burgundy*, 2004. Directed by Adam McKay.

These verses are severe and serious. Jesus, master of the feast and provider of gallons of celebratory aged wine, is now using a whip to drive animals out of the temple. Oxen are mooing, sheep are bleating and pigeons are flapping around all over the place. Moneychangers are scrabbling around, trying to pick up the coins that have been tipped onto the floor. It is a chaotic, undignified scramble. Jesus is on the rampage.[2]

Okay, so where's the funny? We're coming to that.

Light and shade

Truly great comedy requires light and shade. In a nation-wide poll for Britain's Best Sitcom in 2003, the winner was *Only Fools and Horses*. This is a magnificent show, containing wonderfully memorable set-piece scenes like the chandelier incident, Del falling through the bar and the Batman and Robin rescue. But these moments only work because we really care about Del and Rodney. They love each other, and drive each other mad. It isn't just joke after joke. The best comedy is normally underpinned by the best drama.

Back at the temple in John 2, there has been no shortage of drama. Jesus is challenged on his actions, as you'd expect. Verse 18 says:

The Jews therefore answered him, 'What sign do you show us, seeing that you do these things?'

---

2 Sidenote: You could argue there's a continuum with two extremes of Christianity. At one end is the kind that cannot imagine Jesus or God ever being angry, as if the wrath of God simply can't be. At the other end is the kind that has zero problem imagining Jesus being angry and can't imagine Jesus laughing. How can these be reconciled?

What sort of a question is that? What possible thing could Jesus do to satisfy his interrogators? To them, the temple is not just sacred and holy; it is the very dwelling place of Yahweh. Jesus uses this to escalate the situation and present them with a big, red nuclear button.

How do you like them apples?

At such a moment, you might be tempted to take a step back and cool things down. Not Jesus. He is all in. How about this for a request to show his power? 'Destroy this temple, and in three days I will raise it up.' Or:

Hey, priests! Lovely, precious, sacred temple you've got here. Such a shame if anything should happen to it. How about I pull it all down, turn it into rubble and rebuild it? Would you like to see that?

Whoa. That's an *Anchorman* meme moment. That really got out of hand *fast*.

Jesus isn't talking about the actual temple. Although he kind of is. His body is the new temple, which will render the building they are standing in obsolete. The irony is that he is going to destroy the temple with his body when the temple curtain will be torn in two. And then the Romans will destroy it physically in AD 70.

What could the temple priests say to Jesus? Do they feel lucky? Should they call his bluff? What they come out with is typical of the reactions of the elites throughout the rest of John's Gospel. They take him literally. We see Nicodemus do this in the next chapter when he is told to be born

24

again and he starts talking about the biological impossibility. Duh.

Likewise, the priests explain to Jesus how many years it took to build the temple[3] and the practical difficulties of rebuilding in only three days. They don't get it.

The kicker

Rounding off this section, though, is another little joke. John goes on to explain that 'many believed in his name when they saw the signs that he was doing' (John 2.23, ESV). Clearly, after this encounter, Jesus does all kinds of wonderful and miraculous things off to one side. But when he is challenged to produce them at the behest of the elites who are used to being obeyed, he will not do it.

Jesus is not a puppet to be controlled or a puppy to be petted. C. S. Lewis's saviour figure in *The Chronicles of Narnia* is a lion. Based on John 2, that seems about right.

CRSO

---

3   We will glide over the fact that this temple was built with the cooperation of the God-hating, infanticidal King Herod.

The great I AM

I don't know if I've seen *The Ten Commandments* all the way through, but I feel like I have. This box-office block-buster from 1956 conjures up images of important people looking serious. When Moses (Charlton Heston) encounters the burning bush, it's so serious and earnest it's almost comic, which is not far from the original text. Read Exodus 3—4 and you will see a very odd scene in which God repeatedly sends Moses back to Egypt to rescue his people, and Moses isn't having any of it.

Moses offers up excuse after excuse. In Exodus 4.1, he pleads that no one will take him seriously.

> Moses answered, 'But, behold, they will not believe me, nor listen to my voice; for they will say, "Yahweh has not appeared to you."'

God tells Moses to throw his stick onto the ground, which then turns into a snake. What does Moses do? He runs away. I don't know if you can imagine a burning bush holding its head in its hands, but that's the picture we're looking at.

Eventually, Moses offers a sicknote, claiming some kind of speech impediment, to which Yahweh replies, 'Who made man's mouth? Or who makes one mute, or deaf, or seeing, or blind? Isn't it I, Yahweh? Now therefore go, and I will be with your mouth, and teach you what you shall speak' (Exodus 4.11–12).

To which Moses replies, 'Oh, Lord, please send someone else.'

Wow. Moses, you just told God to jog on.

As we read on in Scripture, the vast majority of the 'heroes' are deeply flawed with feet of clay, hearts of stone and brains of mush. We see that vividly in the New Testament with the twelve disciples who, if described on a film blurb, would be called a 'ragtag[1] team of underdogs'.

But this divine encounter is better known for being the moment when God reveals his name. When Moses grovels, 'When I come to the children of Israel, and tell them, "The God of your fathers has sent me to you," and they ask me, "What is his name?" what should I tell them?' (Exodus 3.13). Or, in other words, 'Who shall I say is calling?'

Then God says, 'I AM WHO I AM . . . You shall tell the children of Israel this: "I AM has sent me to you."'

God then speaks at length and in detail about how he is going to turn the tables on the Egyptians and give the Israelites a land flowing with milk and honey. To which Moses says, 'They won't believe me' (Exodus 4.1). Apparently, Moses has a clearer, more accurate vision of the future than the God of Abraham, Isaac and Jacob. It should make you cringe.

The point is this: I AM is revealed as the name of Israel's one true God. So when Jesus makes a statement beginning 'I AM', it's pretty clear that he's making some big claims. In the Moses story, Jesus isn't Moses. He's the burning bush.

I AM so much more

In John's Gospel, Jesus drops the 'I AM' bombshell in John 8.58, saying that he was before Abraham. But he also uses the

---

1 The word 'ragtag' is only ever used in film or sitcom descriptions in this way.

'I AM' phrase for things like, 'I AM the bread of life,' or, 'I AM the door' (John 6.35; 10.9).

As usual, Jesus' opponents keep taking him literally. To be fair to his opponents, what are they to make of Jesus saying, 'I am the good shepherd' (John 10.11)? He literally isn't a shepherd. He is from a family of carpenters in Nazareth. Or so they think.

Jesus' birth in Bethlehem is only mentioned once in John's Gospel (7.42), and there's heavy irony around it. In a sitcom script, it would read like this:

EXT. TEMPLE COURTS. DAY.

[JESUS *is standing on a plinth, preaching.* PHILIP *and* NATHANAEL *are also facing the crowd, looking around nervously.*]

JESUS If anyone is thirsty, let him come to me and drink! He who believes in me, as the Scripture has said, from within him will flow rivers of living water.

PHILIP [*leaning in to* NATHANAEL] Nice Zechariah reference there. Did you get that? Although this might be more Jeremiah. Jesus, when you say, 'living wat—'

[PHILIP *looks round and* JESUS *has gone. The crowd is in uproar.* PHILIP *sees a* TEMPLE PRIEST *holding a rock, looking disappointed. He has really big head gear and looks very intelligent.*]

BYSTANDER 1 This is truly a prophet!

BYSTANDER 2 This is the Christ!

TEMPLE PRIEST [*smug*] Er, I really don't think so. This Jesus comes from Galilee?

NATHANAEL Ha, yeah. And when I first heard about him, I said—

[PHILIP *gives* NATHANAEL *a 'leave it' gesture – and points towards the rock the* TEMPLE PRIEST *is holding.* NATHANAEL *backs away.*]

TEMPLE PRIEST The Scripture clearly says the Christ will be a direct descendant of King David! And born in Bethlehem. So there is just no way this man can be the Christ! Find me the son of a shepherd, who has also not inherited the sin of Adam, presumably by some kind of miraculous divine birth, and I'll believe. Good day to you!

[*The* TEMPLE PRIEST *stomps off.* PHILIP *considers going after him, looks to camera as if to say, 'Shall I tell him?' and then shrugs, and walks off with* NATHANAEL.]

John knows that we know where Jesus was really born, because his Gospel assumes we know the other Gospels.

The good shepherd

So when Jesus says, 'I am the good shepherd', what are people like the temple priest meant to think? Jesus is a carpenter. In fact, Jesus' record with animal herding is, at best, mixed. When Jesus drove a legion of demons out of a man (Mark 5), he allowed the spirits into a herd of pigs who promptly ran into the sea and drowned.[2] The locals begged him to take his 'pig-herding skills' elsewhere. If anyone came to me with that track record, I could be forgiven for not entrusting them with my flock of sheep.

Jesus also says he is the vine and the gate (John 15.1; 10.9, NIV). He is those things. And he isn't. Not literally. So let's cut these folks some slack. Which is why I wrote this:

Earlier manuscripts do not include the following

Jesus began to speak in parables and he said to them, 'Ask and it will be given to you; seek and you will find. Knock and the door will be opened to you.'

Then Peter said, 'Teacher, are you the door on which we are to knock?'

Before Jesus could answer, Nathanael said, 'Is this about doing door-to-door evangelism again?'

Then James said, 'I thought you said you were the gate.'

Jesus said, 'I AM the gate.'

'So, we knock on the gate?' said James. 'Can you knock on a gate?

'Technically?'

'You can rattle it,' said Nathanael.

Peter attempted to clarify. 'Knock on the door or rattle the gate and it will be opened to you.'

'Is it a narrow gate?' said James.

'Look, will you just shut up about gates?' said Peter.

'Well, Matthew's always saying we're supposed to enter through the narrow gate,' said James.

---

2 Mark 5.1–20 and Luke 8.26–39 – but not John. Jesus doesn't drive out any demons in John's Gospel. At all.

'Please stop talking,' said Philip.

'Well, excuse me for not wanting to take the broad road to destruction,' said James.

'Right,' said Peter, again attempting to clarify. 'What we've learnt is that Jesus stands at the door and knocks. And if anyone hears his voice and opens the door, he will come in to eat with us, and us with him. No, that's not right.'

'I like it, though,' said John. 'Might go in my sequel.'

'You're planning a sequel to a book you've not even written yet?' said Peter.

'Can we get back to this metaphor?' said James. 'Jesus is telling us to stand at the door and knock.'

'So we're both knocking on doors? That's a bit weird,' said Peter.

'No,' said Philip. 'There's only one door.'

'We're both knocking on the same door?' said Peter 'Sorry, I've lost track. What side of the door am I on?'

'Jesus is telling us to stand at the door and knock,' said Philip.

'Or rattle the gate,' said James.

'Shut up!' said Peter.

Jesus looked at them and loved them and said, 'Do you still not understand?'

And the disciples said, 'No.'

This is not the word of the Lord.
Thanks be to God.

☙❧

We're no different from these disciples. Christians have always struggled with metaphors. In fact, one of the greatest, most read and most significant works in the English language is meant to be a great allegory. But here's the irony. It literally isn't an allegory. It's about the broad road that leads to destruction and the importance of entering through the narrow gate. And in this fictional world, there really is a broad road and a narrow gate and a character called Christian. Not Bernard, Steve or Trudy. Christian. In short, we need to talk about Bunyan.

Pilgrim's Progress

Or: Why I can't stand one of the
greatest works of Christian writing
in the English language

Maybe it's just me. But I don't get it. Christians love *Pilgrim's Progress*.[1] No one has a bad word to say about it. Except me.

It's touted as an allegory. But it isn't. Christian, burdened by his cares and worries, meets a character called Evangelist. He is literally helped out of the Slough of Despond by someone called Help and he literally goes through the Wicket Gate on his way to the Celestial City, which sits on Mount Zion. This is not an allegory. Aslan is an allegory. Gandalf, Aragorn and Frodo are allegorical types of Christ – the prophet, the king and the suffering servant. *Pilgrim's Progress* is not an allegory. It is, at best, theological fiction.

For me, the literalness of *Pilgrim's Progress* renders it pointless. There is no subtext. We have a sense of what Obstinate, Pliable and Mr Worldly Wiseman are going to do the moment we meet them. The giant's main problem is not a mystery since his name is Despair.

Clearly there is a market for this sort of thing. John Bunyan must have done something right. His book is stupendously

---

1 J. I. Packer, the great evangelical writer who would be canonized if Reformed people went in for that sort of thing, says that Christians should read *Pilgrim's Progress* every year. Nope.

successful by any metric. Since its publication in 1677, it has been told and retold, produced and reproduced, paraphrased, animated, dramatized and rewritten so that tens of millions have heard or read the story, and hundreds of millions have been influenced by it accordingly.

This success says more about Christians than the work itself. Historically, at least, many Christians, especially evangelicals like me, have found it easier and more comforting when things are literal and leave little to the imagination. But this is the mistake we see the disciples and Jesus' enemies making in the Gospels again and again.

All this is a preamble to my own version of *Pilgrim's Progress* which is, essentially, a parody of this great work that has clearly helped and blessed millions. So that probably says more about me than the work itself. But judge for yourself.

Christian makes new friends

In the distance, Christian could just make out the glow of the Celestial City. Fixing his eyes on the light, he was able to make it across the Plain of Distraction. The City was harder to see as he walked through the Woods of Leisurely Pursuits and emerged into the Playing Fields of Eternal Football Matches That Had Gone to Penalties So You Might as Well Watch to the End.

Christian was just settling down to watch one of these games when he remembered the words of his friend Memorable: 'Keep going to the Celestial City.' The words themselves were not memorable, but the man's name was pretty memorable, since it was actually Memorable, so he remembered that quite easily. Memorable had a friend called Mnemonic, who talked quite a lot and seemed more trouble than he was worth. There was another man called Eminently Forgettable but Christian couldn't quite remember if he'd met him or not.

As Christian walked away from the Playing Fields of Eternal Football Matches, he came across three men.

'Hello,' said Christian. 'I'm on my way to the Celestial City.'

'Oh, that sounds great,' said the first man. 'I'm really happy for you.' His name was Sarcastic.

'Thank you,' said Christian, unaware of the man's name and therefore his primary characteristic. 'I am glad to be heading towards the Celestial City.'

'He's joking,' said the second man. 'His name is Sarcastic.'

'I see,' said Christian. 'What is your name?'

(Beat.)

'Suspense,' said the second man.

Just then, Christian saw that Suspense was holding a large, oddly shaped, heavy bag.

'What's in the bag?' asked Christian.

'Secrets,' said Suspense, with an enigmatic smile.

'Secrets? Is that name of a person?' asked Christian, worried that Suspense may be a murderer.

'Wouldn't you like to know?' said Suspense.

'It's not a dead body,' said the third man. His name was Spoilers.

'It's just some bits of wood and he's trying to be all mysterious,' Spoilers went on.

'Oh,' said Christian, a little perturbed. He'd not met people like this before – people who talk like normal people. All of a sudden, he longed to be back with friends he'd made earlier in his journey, people like Plain Speaking, Crystal Clear and Face Value.

At that moment, a fourth man appeared.

'So glad you could join us,' said Sarcasm.

'Were you ever going to tell me where you were or were you just too busy to let me know?' said the fourth man. His name was Passive Aggressive.

Christian decided it was time to be on his way.

'Good luck on your quest to the Celestial City,' said Sarcasm.

'Many more adventures await,' said Suspense.

'Yeah, don't worry. You do make it in the end,' said Spoilers.

'Will you stop doing that?' said the other three as Christian continued on his way, feeling reassured that he was on the Road of Zero Subtext to the Town of Limited Creativity. He could literally not imagine what he would find there.

 CRSO

The truth about the
Good Samaritan

D eath and taxes are not the only certainties in this
world.[1] Another is that every year, during the
Conservative Party Conference, left-wing commen-
tators say that the Tories have taken a 'lurch to the right'.

Another certainty is that no matter what the forthcoming
election is, it is always somehow 'the most important election for a generation'. And even though the results in most
constituencies in the UK and most states in the USA can be
predicted without even the need for opinion polls, your vote
is, apparently, more crucial now than ever.

On social media, people who love politics will insist that in
this election you really can't vote for the party you'd normally
vote for because the leader is a philanderer, a Russian spy or
a communist. Or possibly all three. No matter what happens,
the right-wing politician is labelled a fascist, and the left-wing
politicians are accused of believing in a fantasy money-tree.

All the above is even more tiresome when it's run through
Christian filters, and we're invited to consider who Jesus
would vote for. Jesus, of course, doesn't vote for anyone. Nor
does he ask anyone to vote for him. As Dr S. M. Lockridge
said in his memorable words about Jesus Christ being King

---

1 'In this world, nothing is said to be certain, except death and taxes' is
normally attributed to Benjamin Franklin in 1789, but Daniel Defoe talks
about the certainty of death and taxes in his *The Political History of the Devil*
in 1726.

of Kings and Lord of Lords, 'You can't impeach him and he's not gonna resign.'[2]

Read the Gospels and you will find that attempts to draw Jesus into talking politics simply don't work. He never takes the bait. Like a judo black belt, he always turns the weight of the attacker against them.

None of this stops us from using our favourite verses from the Bible as weapons in political fights. Few have been used and abused more than the story of the Good Samaritan, whose example can be used to promote higher taxes, foreign aid, corn subsidies and whatever cause you can think of.

No one asks what the Good Samaritan thinks. We only see him helping a man who's been robbed and left for dead. But what would happen if he were to meet someone else?

Maybe we'd see his true colours.

Earlier manuscripts do not include the following

To a lawyer asking, 'Who is my neighbour?', Peter told this parable:

'A certain man on a journey fell among robbers, who stripped him, beat him and departed, leaving him half dead. A priest going down that way saw him and passed by on the other side. A Levite also did the same. But then came a Samaritan, who saw the man half dead, or half alive, depending on how you look at it, and was moved with compassion. He came to him, bound up his wounds, poured on oil and wine, set him on his own

---

2 Lockridge, who died in 2000, issued a moving six-minute description of Jesus known as 'That's My King!', which can be heard in many places on the internet such as here: <https://youtu.be/1LT7mQda14s> (accessed 29 January 2021).

animal, brought him to an inn and took care of him. The next day, he paid the innkeeper and said to him, "Take care of him. Let him use the minibar and the spa. I will repay you when I return."

'And so the story of this Samaritan's kindness was told far and wide, much to the annoyance of the chief priests and the teachers of the law who thought Samaritans were just the worst. Which is kind of the point.'

Then the lawyer said to Peter, 'So what you're saying is, the Samaritan—'

'Just wait,' said Peter. 'Don't put words into my mouth, or the mouth of the Samaritan. There's another story.'

And so Peter told another parable:

'Another time, this same Samaritan was on another journey and encountered a young man coming in the other direction. This young man was poor and hungry. At once he recognized the Samaritan.

'"Good Samaritan!" said the young man. "Have mercy on me!"

'"Why do you call me 'Good'?" said the Samaritan.

'"That sounds familiar," said the young man. "Anyway, can you spare any denarii? I need to get to Jericho and all my stuff's been nicked and apparently you have oil and wine and—"

'"Can I stop you there?" said the Good Samaritan. "You know the commandments. Do not give false testimony. Do not steal. Do not defraud . . ."

'"Is that one of them?" said the young man. "I don't remember that."

'"Perhaps you should tell me what really happened," said the Samaritan.

'The young man sighed. "Okay, fine," he said. "My father owns land, and one day I went to him and said, 'Father, give me my share of your property.'"

"'Whoa, really?" said the Samaritan. "Let me get this straight. Effectively, you said, 'Dad, I can't wait 'til you're dead so can I have my inheritance now?'"

"'Don't be like that," said the young man. "I was just trying to branch out, mostly to get away from my big brother who is about as much fun as fasting while being stoned with small rocks."

"'I know that type," said the Samaritan.

"'I know, right?" said the young man. "My dad realized this and gave me my share."

"'And the fact you're walking along this road in rags, looking very hungry, would suggest you squandered these precious resources on riotous living?" said the Samaritan.

"'You have no right to judge me like that," said the young man. "After all, judge not lest ye be judged."

"'I don't think that means what you think it means," said the Samaritan. "We all make judgements all the time, but returning to you and your prodigal habits . . ."

"'Prodigal? Who are you calling 'prodigal'?" said the young man. "What right do you have to call me 'prodigal'?"

"'You don't know what 'prodigal' means, do you?" said the Samaritan.

"'No," said the young man. "I don't. What does it mean?"

"'Wasteful. Extravagant," said the Samaritan.

"'Oh, right," said the young man.

'"Profligate. Wanton."

'"Fine,"' said the young man.

'"Reckless," said the Samaritan.

'"All right! Okay! Look, I may have thrown a few parties in foreign lands," said the young man, seeking to justify himself, "but that's my decision. I'm just being authentic to myself."

'"That's a shame."

'"That's what I've always been taught to be."

'"And how's that been working out for you long term?" said the Samaritan.

'"You're supposed to be the Good Samaritan, but you know what? You're not looking all that 'Good' right now," said the young man.

'"I never claimed to be 'Good'. That's for others to say. All I did was help a guy who'd been beaten up. I did what anyone would have done. Except people who misinterpret laws so they can walk past someone who's dying."

'"I'm dying!" said the young man.

'"No, you're not," said the Samaritan. "You're hungry because you're foolish."

'"No, you are," said the young man.

'"Nice comeback," said the Samaritan. "For it is written, 'It is a fool's pleasure to do wickedness, but wisdom is a man of understanding's pleasure.'"

'"Where does it say that?" said the young man.

'"It is the wisdom of King Solomon himself. Granted wisdom by God," said the Samaritan. "It is one of his many proverbs."[3]

---

3 If you really want to know, it's Proverbs 10.23.

"'Wait. You're a Samaritan. You don't consider Proverbs to be part of the Holy Scripture!" said the young man, turning to some passers-by. "Boom. Owned. Watch as young man DESTROYS Samaritan."

"'But you do consider Proverbs to be Holy Scripture," said the Samaritan. "So why do you ignore these words and then grumble when they turn out to be true?"

"'Oh, now you sound like my dad," said the young man.

"'I thought it was your brother who was the problem," said the Samaritan.

"'Look, shut up," said the young man. "Are you going to give me some money or not?"

"'I can do better than that," said the Samaritan. "Go to Samaria where a friend of mine is looking to hire a young man."

"'A job? Some bleeding-heart liberal you turned out to be," said the young man. "Mind you, if it pays well and is indoors, with five weeks' paid holiday, I'll look at it, especially if I could work from home a few days a week. Although if there's a subsidized canteen, maybe I'll come in. Plus, offices are fun for flirting and—"

"'It comes with accommodation which is 'authentically rustic', and the job is very much part of the free-range and organic economy," said the Samaritan.

"'Oh. So I'd be looking after animals and sleeping in a barn?"

"'Yep. You'd be looking after pigs."

"'Pigs?" said the young man. "They're unclean!"

"'You know, I don't think the pigs will be all that wild about you, either. Despite having cloven hooves and being classified unclean and liking mud, they're actually very clean animals. And intelligent," said the Samaritan. "I think it'll do you good. As you watch the pigs eat their pods, you might learn a few things. It'll be character-building."

'"Now you really sound like my dad," said the young man. "Mind you, if I manage to turn things around, it'll be a really good low point in my story. People love a good testimony, don't they?"

'"They do," said the Samaritan. "Make your way to Nablus and ask for Steve. Say that I sent you."

'"Fine," said the young man, who went on his way.

'"You're welcome," said the Samaritan.

'"I didn't say 'thank you'," said the young man.

'"I know," said the Samaritan, who went on his way muttering about the youth of today.'

Then Peter turned to the lawyer who was listening to this parable and said, 'Who was a neighbour to the young man?'

'Are we still on that?' said the lawyer.

'You're the one who asked a question about your neighbour,' said Peter.

'Did I? To be honest, I was just trying to catch you out and find a loophole,' said the lawyer. 'That's lawyers for you. And this is a sketch so we play up to stereotypes. But I can't help feeling that second parable was very politically motivated.'

'Isn't it just distinguishing between the deserving and undeserving poor?' said Peter.

'I'm not sure that's a helpful distinction,' said the lawyer. 'We're all sinners. Don't the Scriptures repeatedly say, "The Lord is gracious, merciful, slow to anger and of great loving kindness"?'

'Yeah, they do,' said Peter, scratching his head. 'And yet the Proverbs repeatedly commend the virtue of hard work and faithfulness.'

'True,' said the lawyer. 'It's almost like we need the full counsel of Scripture in our lives, rather than grabbing verses that justify our predetermined, emotionally charged political opinions.'

'I don't think that's going to catch on,' said Peter. 'Anyway, this has been fun.'

'In its own way,' said the lawyer.

And they went on their way, wondering what this could mean.

This is not the word of the Lord.
Thanks be to God.

ଓଞ

Walking on the water

Water is miraculous. If you want to see evidence of a creator, look no further than water. If it were to behave like virtually any other compound it would have killed all life on earth centuries ago. When it freezes, it doesn't contract. It expands. And it doesn't get heavier and sink. It floats when frozen. This one property alone means that the life in a lake isn't eviscerated by the coming of winter, or the entire planet permanently covered in ice.

Water also has unusually high surface tension, which means that some insects can walk on it. But not humans. Except one. As miracles go, Jesus walking on the water is an odd one, since it's not healing someone or providing for a felt need. And at the time, it would have been creepy. The disciples shriek, 'It's a ghost!' But Peter reacts very differently: 'Lord, if it's you, tell me to come to you on the water.' This is perhaps the oddest moment of the whole scene. I've often wondered what John and the other disciples said about this afterwards. Here's a version:

Earlier manuscripts of Matthew's Gospel do not include the following

While Jesus went off to pray alone, the disciples sat by the shore of the lake. Peter was drying his clothes.

'So,' said John, 'talk me through what just happened.'

'Our Lord walked on water,' said Peter.

'Shades of crossing the Jordan?' said Andrew.

'Or the parting of the Red Sea?' said James.

'Is there a bit with Elijah doing something similar?' said Nathanael.

'Maybe it goes back even further, to God and the firmament, you know, in the beginning,' said John.

'Why don't you put it in your book, John?' said Peter.

'I probably will,' said John. 'But I'm still trying to get my head around what you said to Jesus in the boat just now.'

'You're wondering why I didn't join in with you lot shrieking, "Argh! A ghost!"' said Peter.

'Wow,' said John. 'Are we doing this?'

'Doing what?' said Peter.

'Playing "Which disciple looked the most stupid?"' said John.

And Peter said to him, 'Fine. I'll go first. You saw someone who looked exactly like Jesus, who had literally just fed thousands of people with five loaves and two fish, so the laws of physics basically do not apply, and you concluded that this was the ghost of someone who is still alive. Cos that's a thing.'

'Excuse me for being surprised at seeing someone walking on water,' said John. 'You do know that people can't generally walk on water? Although maybe that explains why you packed in fishing. You don't really seem to understand how water actually works.'

'Ouch,' said Andrew. 'Peter's a good fisherman and you know it.'

'Okay. Fine. That was unnecessary,' said John. 'Maybe we should've realized it was just Jesus walking on the water. But none of us did what you did next, did we?'

'I may have bitten off a little more than I could chew,' said Peter, sheepishly.

'A little more?' said John. 'You went nuts. You said to Jesus walking on the water, "Hey, my turn! Lord, tell me to come to you on the water!" What a bizarre reaction. When Jesus changed water into wine, did you think, "I should be able to do that. Pass me a jug"?'

'You say that, but I did actually walk on the water,' said Peter.

'And how did that go?' said John. 'After a few steps, you saw the wind and the waves and—'

Peter interrupted, 'Did I or did I not walk on water?'

'Yes,' said John. 'But you also sank like a stone. Ha, is that why Jesus calls you "the Rock"?'

And the disciples had a good laugh.

'Fine. Yak it up,' said Peter. 'But just bear in mind that someone here walked on water. Which one of us was that? Was it John, the disciple whom Jesus loves? Or me? Simon Peter. The idiot fisherman. You know what? They might even sing a song about me. "Simon Peter walks on water. Tra-la-la-la-la la-la-la-la!"'

'They won't sing that about you,' said John.

'They might,' said Peter.

'You sank,' said John. 'And you didn't just sink. You cried out, "Lord, save me!" It was, well, a bit pathetic. I didn't know where to look.'

'I did,' said Nathanael. 'I watched you nearly drown. It was hilarious!'

'Yeah,' admitted Peter. 'That was a low point. But one of us thought Jesus was a ghost. And one of us walked on water. So, which disciple looked the most stupid?'

'I'm not playing this game,' said John.

'Because you lost,' said Peter.

'Lord, save me!' said John.
'Look, a ghost!' said Peter.
'Shut up,' said John.
'Shut up,' said Peter.

This is not the word of the Lord.
Thanks be to God.

CR80

Interval

I often perform these pieces in churches, and there's usually an interval when people have a glass of something and mill around. So this part of the book is the interval and the tone is a bit different. The next chapter is also the longest.[1] If you read this book in a downstairs loo, you might require two or three sittings, for which I make no apology.[2] I'm trying to explain how I feel about the miracles. It used to be fashionable, especially within my own denomination, the Church of England, to be sceptical about the miracles. And yet somehow, here I am not only attending an Anglican church but also, at the time of writing, a member of the General Synod and the Archbishops' Council. I'd like to explain how that happened. Along the way, I mention *Father Ted* and *The Vicar of Dibley*. It does all come together, I promise. Maybe promote the book to the bedside table for a while and read it in bed.

---

1 Sorry, but I'm a comedy writer, and one of the tricks is about setting the right expectations.
2 At least no apology beyond my instinctive British one of just starting a sentence with 'Sorry', without even realizing you're doing it. Like I just did in that last footnote.

Losing your religion

*Or: How I stayed an Anglican
despite believing in miracles*

> The believers in miracles accept them (rightly or wrongly) because they have evidence for them. The disbelievers in miracles deny them (rightly or wrongly) because they have a doctrine against them.
> *Orthodoxy*, G. K. Chesterton[1]

Autobiographies by Christians often have a chapter about doubts, and those long, dark nights of the soul, extreme tests and suffering, where it felt like God wasn't there, or that this whole Christian story felt like a fabric of interwoven myths, embellishments and politically motivated mind tricks. The title of this chapter would suggest this is my chapter like that.

It isn't. Or at least it's not about *my* doubts. This chapter is about the doubts of others. The chapter title is derived from the mournful song 'Losing My Religion' by REM that was everywhere in the early nineties. It felt like a better title than the first line of the song 'You Sexy Thing' by Hot Chocolate about believing in miracles.

---

1 G. K. Chesterton, *Orthodoxy* (Peabody Massachusetts: Hendrickson Christian Classics, 2006), p. 146.

Do I believe in miracles?

In the Gospel accounts, the miracles of Jesus are rarely questioned or doubted. Even when Lazarus is raised from the dead in John 11, the reports from those who were there are assumed to be true. In fact, they worry that this will make Jesus too popular.

Read the Gospels carefully and you will see that the scepticism of Jesus' enemies comes from a logical standpoint, not a faith one. But it's not the logic that you would expect. It was widely believed that God did not answer the prayers of the unrighteous. Jesus, being an unrighteous, blaspheming, Sabbath-breaker, will not have his prayers answered. System error. Does not compute. Turn off and on again.

That was then. This is now. Do I believe the miracles recounted in the Gospels? Do I believe that Jesus turned water into wine? Did he feed the five thousand people?[2] Did he raise Lazarus from the dead? Yes. Yes. Yes.[3] And yes. I believe in miracles in the Bible without hesitation.[4] I believe that my view has made a resurgence in the Church of England in recent years, as I will explain in a moment. And, in the style of G. K. Chesterton, I would say it's not just possible to believe in miracles, but that it's impossible to not believe in them.

Back in the 1990s

Thirty years ago, many in the church were concluding that they didn't believe in the miracles, or that they were not required. After all, science was growing in its explanatory

---

2 And then four thousand people (Matthew 15.29–39).

3 Yes.

4 The miracles of Benny Hinn, not so much.

power, and sensible, enlightened graduates, including ordained clergy, didn't believe in superstitious nonsense. And once they began to pull on that thread, the whole shroud started to unravel. Not only did they not believe in miracles. They were also losing their religion.

Doubt was everywhere, being continually heaped on the foundations of the Christian story. On the recommendation of my delightful church-going cousin, Simon, I read a book I was assured was a best-seller: *The Holy Blood and the Holy Grail* by Michael Baigent, Richard Leigh and Henry Lincoln. This was the book on which the central conspiracy of the *The Da Vinci Code* was based.[5] Not prone to doubt, I found *The Holy Blood and the Holy Grail* unconvincing, but I figured that, if true, it would probably come up during my theology degree at the University of Durham. It didn't.

With this in mind, in 1994 I chose a course entitled 'The Inter-Testamental Period: With Special Reference to the Dead Sea Scrolls'. I wanted to do the course partly because the lecturer was excellent, but also because other sensationalist paperbacks were now suggesting the writings of the Dead Sea Sect, hushed up by the Vatican, cast even greater doubt on the Christian story. (Long story short: the Dead Sea Sect were a pretty weird bunch who were in no way representative of mainstream Jewish or Christian belief.)

---

5 This is not a complex deduction. One character in the novel has the name 'Teabing', which is pretty weird. And then you realize it's an anagram of the name of *Holy Blood* author, 'Baigent'.

The origins of *Father Ted*

The year 1994 also saw the launch of a couple of brand new sitcoms that are oddly relevant. One, on Channel 4, was called *Paris*. You probably missed it, or don't remember it, mainly because it's rarely repeated, being not very good. On my *Sitcom Geeks* podcast, I had the privilege of speaking to writer Graham Linehan about it,[6] and he explained why. Long story short: they didn't know what they were doing and refused to take notes or change anything.[7] These lessons were learnt and carried over into *Father Ted*, which followed a few years later.[8]

Father Ted was intended to be a vitriolic attack on the Catholic Church, but it was too quirky and affectionate to deliver on that score. We loved Craggy Island, a place where the Catholic Church hid troublemakers, idiots, deviants and drunks.

The faith of Father Ted Crilly is genuine to a point. Does he believe in miracles? Maybe, but he is a vain pragmatist. Sometimes a miracle might need some 'help'. Father Dougal's faith is utterly naïve and often absent, and Father Jack is the whisky priest with other problems. Everyone watching would have been well aware of cases of sexual abuse that had been

---

6 Episode 65, if you're interested. In episode 66, he talks about how much he loves *Seinfeld*.

7 Being slightly geeky for a moment, the plots were essentially too long – and they didn't want to cut anything, which meant they had to make cuts in the edit. At that point, the only way to cut the show down to 26 minutes is to cut jokes, rather than story. If you cut story, it stops making sense. But you can cut jokes, so it makes sense. It just ends up not being very funny. This, ultimately, was the problem of *Paris*.

8 Being a writer myself, I am, of course, much more interested in failure than success. Which is why when Dave Cohen and I interviewed Steven Moffatt for the podcast, the thing I wanted to know about most was not *Sherlock*, *Doctor Who*, *Coupling* or *Press Gang* – but the much-loathed BBC1 sitcom from 1997 set in a school, called *Chalk*. In my defence, failure isn't just more interesting than success. It is also more educative.

coming to light in the mainstream media throughout the 1990s. In short, everything from miracles to the authority of the Catholic Church was being questioned.

The Vicar of Dibley

In 1994, we also saw of the debut of a cosier clerical sitcom set in the Anglican Church. Also a huge hit, *The Vicar of Dibley* centred on a new female vicar. The Church of England had recently allowed women to become priests and this change lent itself to an interesting situation that felt fresh and original. Written by a master of comedy, Richard Curtis,[9] it quickly became a firm favourite of the nation.

Look at church attendance figures and you will see them dropping throughout the 1990s, going from bad to worse, so it may seem odd that the increasingly faithless nation would take *The Vicar of Dibley* to heart. The genius of the show is not that Geraldine (Dawn French) is passionate about Jesus, although her faith is clearly genuine and sincere (along with her love for Sean Bean). Religious faith is not a great emotion in comedy or drama. One main reason for this is that religious motivation is hard to empathize with if you don't have it.

Geraldine's prime motivation isn't for her flock to follow Jesus, but for them to like her.[10] This is why she ends up eating

---

9 The show was the creation of Richard Curtis, but many of the episodes were co-written by a delightful man called Paul Mayhew Archer, who was to turn out to be a very kind mentor to me early in my career. Thank you, Paul.

10 Being kind to Geraldine, we can say she falls into the trap of believing that if people like her, and she likes Jesus, then people will like Jesus and be drawn to him. There is plenty of theology to support this view, but it's often quite painful to watch, and we're back to the trendy vicar who preaches the water into wine miracle as, 'Hey, Jesus loved a party too.'

three Christmas lunches on Christmas Day: because she can't say 'no' to anyone. She's too nice. That's a universal flaw everyone can identify with, even if it is not their own besetting sin. In a way, Geraldine is a female version of the 'Derek Nimmo' type of vicar, which still had some resonance in pop culture in the 1990s.[11]

What was the overall effect of this? Mainstream comedy tends to reflect current attitudes rather than challenge or subvert them,[12] so it wasn't telling the audience anything it either didn't know or hadn't subconsciously suspected. It did perpetuate the view that the Church of England was cosy and reassuring and that the faithful laity, at least, were oddballs.

A common thread

But the regulars in Dibley have one common attribute beyond eccentricity. Alice, Owen, Jim, Frank and Hugo are stupid. Being a sitcom, we shouldn't be surprised at the idiocy of the characters, and I'm not accusing Richard Curtis of implying that only credulous morons are Christians. Geraldine isn't stupid and is clearly well educated. David Horton (Gary Waldhorn) is smart, but he is also a mean misogynist. All the other characters, however, are backward.

Do the members of the congregation in Dibley believe in miracles? Probably. But mainly because they are uneducated or gullible. Those with a graduate degree, the majority

---

11 For more on this type of thing, have a look at Bryony Taylor, *More TV Vicar? Christians on the Telly: The good, the bad and the quirky* (London: Darton, Longman & Todd, 2015) and the later chapter in this book where I mention *All Gas and Gaiters*.
12 Okay, it's a bit more complicated than that. It does nudge them along and there's a bit of feedback loop, but this really is one for another time.

of clergy, all of whom have been to some kind of theological educational setting, know better. After all, how could you be a well-educated modern person and still believe in miracles?

One way out would be to stop being modern and to become post-modern. Revd Anthony Freeman tried this. It didn't quite work out.

Never mind the cassocks

A couple of months before *The Vicar of Dibley* landed on BBC1, a current affairs show called *Here and Now* interviewed a clergyman called Anthony Freeman. He was Priest-in-charge of St Mark's, Staplefield, in West Sussex, until it was clear that he no longer believed in God. He would have explained his position with greater nuance, but essentially he held a post-modern view that God is subjective, and could be found in our hearts, but not reality. He said there should be a place in the Church of England for people like him since 'a substantial number (of priests and vicars) share my views'.[13]

I think we invited him to come and speak at the Durham Union Society. I might have even met him. I remember the story breaking and a picture of him in the press walking along in a black cassock, looking rather dramatic. But the story wasn't a surprising one at the time. When he implied that his kind of scepticism was widespread among the clergy, no one was genuinely shocked. He was only saying out loud what many knew to be the case.

---

13 Glenda Cooper, 'Sacked vicar says many of clergy doubt God exists', *Independent*, 2 August 1994, <www.independent.co.uk/news/uk/sacked-vicar-says-many-of-clergy-doubt-god-exists-1373927.html> (accessed 14 January 2021).

That bishop

This was the time when the even-more-educated elites were prepared to say the unsayable, as the nation continued to lose its religion. The Bishop of Durham, David Jenkins, was throwing doubt on the resurrection of Jesus Christ itself. He did not say it was 'a conjuring trick with bones'. Not quite. He said it 'was *not just* a conjuring trick with bones'.[14] But the presence of the word 'just' in that sentence did not help him as much as he thought.

When this story broke, there was some clutching of pearls in the pews, but no one was surprised that a Church of England bishop should talk like this. He was a highly educated man. And highly educated men know that you do not take the Bible literally. How could you?

Yes we Anglican

So back to me. Given the picture painted by *The Vicar of Dibley* and the statements of Anthony Freeman and a senior bishop, the City of Durham in 1994 was a place of doubt. I was not, and am not, one who doubts the fundamentals of the Christian faith, or the miraculous. So the chances of me becoming any kind of Anglican seemed pretty low.

When I arrived in Durham and was looking for a Sunday service, I'd heard that the church of choice was St Nicholas. This was the Anglican church in the marketplace with a tall spire – although everything in Durham is dwarfed by the cathedral and castle. St Nics appealed to me as it claimed a solid

---

14 Mark Goodacre, 'A conjuring trick with bones', NT Blog, 1 July 2005, <https://ntweblog.blogspot.com/2005/07/conjuring-trick-with-bones.html> (accessed 29 January 2021).

evangelical heritage. In the late 1970s, the vicar of the church had been the famously evangelical George Carey, who had risen to be Archbishop of Canterbury. But he was an outlier. It is said that he was not the choice the Church of England wanted, and that it was the result of the bloody-minded Methodist Prime Minister Margaret Thatcher in her final days choosing the 'wrong' name.[15]

On his appointment to the primacy of England in 1991, George Carey was portrayed by *Spitting Image* as a swivel-eyed, tambourine-banging, 'born-again' Christian who would sometimes say 'Kumbaya'.[16] This was clearly meant to be insulting and satirical. I found it reassuring. Our Archbishop seemed to have a vibrant, biblical, Spirit-filled faith. He believed in miracles. That was a good start. Maybe there was a place for me in the Church of England. I gave St Nics a go.

No we Anglican't

I didn't last long at St Nics. It was okay. But only okay. I don't think anything was wrong, but soon most of my friends from the Christian Union – and a girl I liked at the time – were attending a church up the road led by an excellent Bible teacher and preacher called Bob Fyall, who also lectured at Cranmer Theological College.

This was an unusually evangelical place of worship in the

---

15 Read all about it here: Chris Gray, 'Devious, secretive, but ever so polite: the race is on to lead the Church of England', *Independent*, 7 January 2002, <www.independent.co.uk/news/uk/this-britain/devious-secretive-ever-so-polite-race-lead-church-england-9209215.html> (accessed 14 January 2021).

16 See later chapter for further discussion of 'Kumbaya'.

United Reformed Church, a denomination I'd never heard of. Since then, church history has shown me that the very name 'United Reformed Church' is comic. The odds on anything being both united *and* theologically Reformed are very slim.

Heaven knows I'm an Anglican now

So what has changed since 1994? Why am I an Anglican now? And not just an evangelical who happens to attend a Church of England church, but someone who has stood in elections in the Diocese of Bath and Wells and given many hours and days to read lengthy papers and attend meetings of the General Synod and the Archbishops' Council?

There are many reasons. They begin with the foundational documents and the inspiring history of the reformers who wrote them, like Cranmer, Hooper, Ridley and Latimer. But another reason, oddly, relates to miracles and who believes in them.

Through numerous meetings with ordained and lay leaders of the Church of England, I've almost always encountered genuine, optimistic faith in Jesus Christ. It is the kind of faith that believes in miracles, or at least has an openness to consider them, and takes them seriously.

Three tribes

I should add that the kind of faith espoused by the different tribes within the Church of England is not always something I agree with. For those who aren't aware, there are three main types of churchmanship in the Church of England, which form three main groups within the General Synod. I shall attempt to summarize these in a single paragraph, thereby enraging everyone in equal measure. Here we go:

The evangelicals take the Bible as the supreme authority in all matters and seek to establish the primacy of the preaching of the Word, both for evangelism and discipleship. Next we have the Anglo-Catholics, who see the sacraments and rites as the main way in which Christ is proclaimed and the faith of the Christian is nurtured and encouraged. Then we have the progressives, who may have sympathy with the evangelicals (in fact, many once were) and an affinity for the rituals, but their passion is changing the church and, where necessary, core doctrines in order to be relevant to society.

Each of these has its merits, and on a good day each group would claim to have sympathy for and fellowship with the other two. Each of the groups also has wings of its own and splinter groups. But each group is passionate about its own convictions, and the faith as each understands it is genuine.

Status symbols

My theory, untested and untestable, is this: in the past, up until the 1980s perhaps, people might have been brought up in the Christian faith and, given its special status in society, have pursued a career in the church. This would not bring just status, but also a home, a regular income and the possibility of being a bishop in the House of Lords or the dean of a cathedral. It worked for Cardinal Wolsey, famously the son of a butcher.

But what about having to believe in miracles? Everyone

knows they didn't happen, because they couldn't have. Well, they can be spiritualized or theologized out of existence. Once you get there, making God a concept that dwells in human consciousness is barely a hop, skip and a jump away. Therefore, Anthony Freeman could claim that 'a substantial number (of priests and vicars) share my views'.

Those days are gone, as are those priests and vicars. After all, who'd be a vicar now unless they were highly motivated? It's not a high-status job and hasn't been for decades. It is demanding and exhausting. If you are well educated or have a degree, and since tax bands changed in the 1980s, you could make significantly more money doing virtually anything else, in management, law or business. And if you want to be both well paid *and* highly respected, become a GP. They are the new priest class.

As our society has grown richer, the pay, conditions, pressure and accommodation of stipendiary ministry in the Church of England are no longer attractive to the would-be Anthony Freemans, who look at the remuneration package and perks and discover that they don't believe it half as much as they thought they did. And the likes of David Jenkins might find a home in academia rather than the House of Bishops. That, at least, is my theory. And this is why there is a home for me in the Church of England, a home for an evangelical who believes wholeheartedly in the miracles of Jesus, and his literal resurrection and curious ascension and promised return.

But I don't think I'm unusual. I'm just being honest. I say I believe in miracles because we can't not believe in them. And I'm going to cite one more sitcom in the interval that has taken a slightly serious tone. Don't worry. Jokes will be back soon, once everyone's topped up their drinks and been to the loo.

Crises of faith

Some clergy do have a crisis of faith while in Christian ministry. This doesn't happen as often as TV storylines would suggest.[17] The burdens are high, and the job is potentially endless, especially if you really do believe and want to help people.

If you want to see what that looks like, there's a sitcom for that too, called *Rev*. But while some clergy identified with it, as it addressed the exhausting but lonely job of parish ministry, it was not a mainstream hit. It was not intended to be. It was a window on a world that the mainstream has learned to ignore almost completely: the Church of England.

I found the series frustrating to watch, but I'm not in full-time paid Christian ministry and I'm not plagued by the doubts of the wonderfully named Adam Smallbone who goes on a journey towards doubt and despair.

But even *Rev* shows us a divine, miraculous encounter, during Adam's darkest hour.[18] He meets a nameless character, played by Liam Neeson, who tells Adam that we all have our cross to bear. As the scene unfolds, we are clearly invited to believe that this isn't a homeless man, but Jesus. Adam is having his own transfiguration.

No matter how sceptical we become, even when it tips over into cynicism, we cannot extinguish the hope we have that

---

17 See later chapter for that.
18 Episode 5, Series 3, *Rev* by Tom Hollander and James Woods, BBC2. First aired 21 April 2014.

sometimes God breaks through into our reality and does something we thought impossible. That's what a miracle is. It is a sign of hope. And hope is something we can never extinguish. If we're honest, we must admit that *not* believing in miracles is the most intolerable burden.

[*Interval over. Lights are going down. Careful where you put your glass. Don't kick it over.*]

છઠ્ઠ૦

For it is written, right?

German is great language. It's not pretty, but it's brilliant. It is the Lego of languages. You can snap words together and make new words. My favourite German assembly of words is probably *Freizeitmöglichkeiten*, which literally means 'free time possibility things', i.e. things you do in your spare time. I don't know what the German for 'making up words in your spare time' is, but I suspect they could do it all in one word. You've got to admire that.

The Germans also have words for concepts that we enjoy or experience but don't have words for. The most obvious is *Schadenfreude*, which means 'the enjoyment of the misfortune of others'. This is now an English word. In my opinion, this isn't enough. We need an English word for enjoying the misfortune of a German.

But we have other things for which we don't have words, but should. I'd love a word for offering to help someone while hoping he or she will say 'no'. I've invented a few words of my own that might be useful in a church context. And so I present to you 'Luxauslandiphobia', which is the fear that God might give you a dramatic vision that he wants you to be a missionary in a foreign country. A more pressing need might be the word 'Dreivierphobia', which you may have experienced during a church-based seminar. It is the fear that you are about to be broken into groups of three or four to discuss some questions.

I mention all this because I feel we need a word for the nod you give when people refer to a passage of the Bible or a part of church history that they think you would know, but you have no idea what they're talking about. So you give a nod of the head, to give the impression that you get the reference.

If we invent a word for that, it should be based on an Aramaic word, since I suspect the disciples nodded their heads as if they knew what Jesus was talking about quite a lot. Jesus is often quoting Scripture, saying, 'For it is written' or, 'The Scriptures say', implying that we should know this.

But what happens when we look up those references in the Old Testament? Sometimes they don't quite match. There are good theological and cultural reasons for this, and it would be wrong to hold Gospel writers to the same standards as twenty-first-century publishing, expecting footnotes[1][2] and bibliographies.[3]

Early manuscripts do not include the following

A young ruler came up to the disciples and said, 'Is Jesus around?'

'No,' said James. 'He has gone to a solitary place to pray.'

'When will he be back?' said the young ruler.

'How should I know?' said James. 'Am I my brother's keeper?'

'Ooh, nice reference,' said Peter. He turned to the young ruler and said, 'That's Cain in Genesis, isn't it?'

---

1   No one reads footnotes.
2   Unless, of course, they're at the bottom of the page. In which case you sometimes do, but then wish you hadn't as it ruins the flow. Like I am in this footnote which is clearly going on too long, without adding any extra information, but is at least demonstrating the idea that your brain is now disengaged with the original purpose of this chapter. What is the purpose? Is it another one about parables? It's okay, you can stop reading now.
3   Ha. Made you look.

'Yeah, I get it,' said the young ruler. 'Although it makes it sound like you've killed your brother. Which I presume you haven't.'

'Our Lord is the Son of Man who raises people from the dead,' said Peter. 'You think he can be killed?'

'I dunno. You're the disciple. I'm just some rich dude seeking wisdom. When will Jesus be back? I'm on a bit of deadline here.'

'Oh, so sorry that the Son of God isn't available at the moment,' said James.

'There's no need to be like that,' said the young ruler. 'You two'll have to do, I suppose.'

'Charming,' said James.

'So here's the thing,' said the young ruler. 'What must I do to be saved?'

'It is written,' said Peter, '"Do not murder," "Do not commit adultery," "Do not steal," "Do not give false testimony," and, erm . . . I can never remember the other ones.'

'"Honour your father and mother"?' said James.

'Yes. Good. How many's that?' said Peter, counting on his fingers.

'Isn't there one about the Sabbath?' said the rich young ruler.

'Oh yeah. And it is written, "Do not defraud",' said James.

'I don't remember that one,' said Peter.

'Is that in there? Or did I imagine it?' said James. He looked at the rich young ruler, who shrugged.

'Feels like it overlaps with stealing,' said the rich young ruler.

'Well, you're the rich young ruler,' said James.

'I'm not rich because other people are poor,' said the rich young ruler. 'That's not how it works.'

'You would say that, wouldn't you?' said James.

'Ah, let me tell another parable about the Good Samaritan,' said Peter.

'No, thanks. Can we get back to my question? And these commandments – didn't we miss out the most important one, about having no other gods?'

'Ah yes! Well, there you go,' said Peter.

'No, not, "There you go." Who is the one true God?' said the rich young ruler. 'Is it Jesus or should I wait for another?'

And Peter said, 'As it is written in Isaiah the prophet, "Behold, I send my messenger before your face, who will prepare your way before you. The voice of one crying in the wilderness, 'Make ready the way of the Lord. Make his paths straight!'"'

'Ah yes,' said James, nodding his head as if he knew what Peter was referring to.

'Okay, is anyone actually checking these references?' said the rich young ruler.

Now a teacher of the law was standing by and said, 'That's not what Isaiah actually says. I know for a fact that half of that quote is from Malachi.'

'If you must know,' sighed Peter, 'that verse is a composite text on a redemptive trajectory.'

'What does that mean?' said James.

'I have no idea,' said Peter. 'I read it in a commentary. But it sounds clever, doesn't it?'

'Hello?' said the rich young ruler. 'Trying to get to heaven here?'

James, the brother of Jesus, looked at the man and

loved him. 'You don't have, because you don't ask,' he said. 'You ask, and don't receive, because you ask with wrong motives, so that you may spend it on your pleasures. You adulterers and adulteresses, don't you know that friendship with the world is hostility toward God? Whoever therefore wants to be a friend of the world makes himself an enemy of God. Or do you think that the Scripture says in vain, "The Spirit who lives in us yearns jealously"?'

'Okay, you've just made that one up,' said the teacher of the law. 'The Scripture at no point talks about the Spirit yearning jealously.'

'Well, it's the gist of the Old Testament!' said James.

'Oh, we're into gists now, are we?' said the teacher of the law. 'And FYI it is not the gist of the Old Testament.'

'Like you'd know!' said James. 'You're one of the people plotting to kill my brother. Talk about missing the point!'

Peter said to the rich young ruler, 'Look, can we get back to you? Jesus might be free at the ninth hour but I can't make any promises.'

At this his face fell, for he had a very busy schedule.

'I'll try to move some things around,' he said.

'It is written,' said James, '"There is a time for meeting and a time for moving things around."'

'Ecclesiastes?' said Peter.

'Give or take,' said James.

This is not the word of the Lord.
Thanks be to God.

CRSO

Evangelistic strategies

In 2015, I had the honour of being elected to represent the Diocese of Bath and Wells at the General Synod. As a result, for five years I was automatically an *ex officio* member of my Deanery and Diocesan Synods. Put simply, I go to a lot of meetings about church that technically aren't actually church.

Maybe it's a denominational thing, but I will say this: Anglicans love sticky notes. If you're running a meeting and worried that it's going to be boring, break the room into groups and hand out sticky notes. Have people brainstorm ideas for the latest iteration of the Deanery Mission Strategy or Diocesan Community Engagement Initiative. It soaks up half an hour. Everyone writes things on sticky notes, which are then placed on flip charts, collected up and never seen again.

This happens so often and is done with such conviction that it isn't a massive waste of time or meeting filler that I've assumed it must be commanded by a bit of Scripture I haven't read for a long time. Maybe it's hanging around at the end of 2 Chronicles where Hezekiah brainstorms ideas for fixing up the temple. Maybe it's commanded in Jude's letter – which is so weird, no one ever reads past verse 9, in which we're told the Archangel Michael argues with the devil about the body of Moses (I kid you not). But I checked both of those places and it's not there.

Then I did some digging and found some early drafts of John's Gospel – which in turn explain why there is no Sending Out of the Twelve or the Seventy that we find in the other

Gospels. In fact, John doesn't even list the twelve disciples.[1] This is what I found:

Earlier manuscripts of John include the following, which is omitted from later, more authoritative versions
Now after these things, the Lord also appointed seventy others, and sent them two by two ahead of him into every city and place where he was about to come. Then he said to them, 'The harvest is indeed plentiful, but the labourers are few. Pray therefore to the Lord of the harvest, that he may send out labourers into his harvest. Go your ways. Behold, I send you out as lambs among wolves. Carry no purse, nor wallet, nor sandals. Greet no one on the way. Into whatever house you enter, first say, "Peace be to this house."'

The seventy went on their way, and immediately called another meeting.

Lucius, one of the seventy, said, 'Eusebius and I aren't quite clear on the plan here. Don't get me wrong. We're excited but I really think we could benefit from a clearer mission statement. Can we brainstorm a few ideas?'

'In a moment,' said Eusebius, 'I'm going to ask everyone to take some sticky notes and write down some ideas, and then we can stick them onto this olive tree and talk about how they make us feel. No right or wrong answers.'

'Our mission statement needs to be seriously punchy,' said Lucius. 'I mean, say what you like about the guy, King Herod's got a really clear mission statement.'

---

1 He's been gathering a few in the first few chapters and doesn't complete the set. Doesn't seem that John's a team player.

'What, "Kill them. Kill them all"?' said Peter.

'Yeah,' said Lucius. 'I mean, it's a bit "killy" for us. But there's good repetition. It's only five words. You've got to admit it's snappy.'

'The temple's slogan is hopeless,' said Simon the Zealot. 'I can't even remember it. Something about being in the community, good rates on money-changing, and humanely incinerating animals. I forget the exact details.'

'Stop!' said Peter. 'This is insane. Were you not listening to Jesus earlier?'

'Actually, I was getting the sticky notes,' said Lucius.

'And I was getting these highlighters,' said Eusebius, with great joy.

'Ooh, we've got highlighters,' said the disciples. And there was much excitement.

But then Peter stood up and said, 'How about this: "Go and make disciples of all nations"?'

'Nah, too vague,' said Lucius. '"All nations"? I mean, what does that even mean?'

'And the concept of a nation state is pretty arbitrary given a united Europe under the Romans,' said Andrew.

'It won't last,' said Simon the Zealot.

'Also, it's strategic overwhelm,' said Lucius. '"Go and make disciples of all nations"? How are the seventy of us going to do that? It's just not going to happen. It needs to be real to people individually.'

'Ooh, ooh, ooh!' said Thaddeus. 'We should tell people that thing Jesus said. When he was talking to Nicodemus.'

'Er, "You must be born again"?' said the disciple whom Jesus loved.

'No, not that. People really won't like the phrase "born again",' said Thaddeus. 'I was thinking about the next bit. After the weird thing about the snake being lifted up.'

'"For God so loved the world that he gave his only son that whoever believes in him shall not perish but have eternal life?"' said John.

'Boom,' said Thaddeus. 'Love that. You could put that on a T-shirt. Mugs. In fact, you know what I'm going to do? I'm going to put it on a sign and hold it up next time I go and watch the gladiators.'

'Ooh, great idea,' said Philip. 'Except you can't get that all on a sign.'

'It's okay,' said Thaddeus. 'I'll just put a reference to it so people can go away and look it up for themselves. In this book of yours, John, what's it going to be? Chapter 3-ish?'

'Yeah, about that,' said John. 'Maybe verse 16. Give or take.'

'Well, that sounds like a plan,' said Lucius. 'Anything else?'

'How about some Christian symbol on the back of a chariot?'

Then Philip said, 'Earlier, when Jesus said we have to say stuff like "Peace be to this house", I worry about being a bit preachy. Wouldn't it be better to not say anything? You know, preach the gospel at all times and if necessary use words?'

'Ooh, yes,' said Lucius. 'I like that.'

'Right. I have to step in here. Jesus uses words,' said Peter.

'Yup. He definitely uses words,' said John.

Matthew agreed.

'I hear you,' said Lucius.

'Yes. Because I used words,' said Peter.

'Yes, but I can tell from your demeanour exactly what you mean,' said Lucius. 'You look like you want to punch me in the face.'

'I do,' said Peter. 'And I will. And if necessary use fists.'

'Sure,' said Lucius, 'but I don't think you really understand how mission works these days?'

'It sounds to me,' said Peter, 'like you just don't want to tell people about Jesus.'

'Anyone can just tell people about Jesus,' said Lucius.

'Apparently not,' said Peter. 'You'd rather rely exclusively on actions.'

'On that,' said Barnabas, 'Clement and I have worked out some really powerful mime which I reckon could be very effective. So when Jesus tells us to enter a house, is he ruling out street theatre?'

Peter replied, 'Jesus said to not greet anyone on the road. So . . .'

'But Barnabas and Clement have worked really hard on this,' said Lucius, 'and I think they should be given a chance to do their thing.'

'No,' said Peter. 'You heard Jesus. Enter a house and say, "Peace be to this house," and—'

'How do we feel about wristbands?' said Lucius. 'I'm thinking WWJD. What Would Jesus Do?'

'No,' said Peter. 'Not, "What Would Jesus Do?" Make some wristbands that say DWJS. Do What Jesus Says.

Repent. Believe. Tell people about the kingdom of God. Make disciples of all nations.'

'Okay. Compromise,' said Lucius. 'Have a look at the street theatre and see what you think.'

And immediately, Barnabas and Clement did their mime. And it was awful.

Lucius said, 'It's pretty weird that the seventy aren't mentioned in the rest of the New Testament. And their names not recorded.'

'I think we now know why,' said Peter.

Lucius said, 'Where's Jesus gone?'

Jesus had gone to a remote place. Alone. To pray. A lot.

This is not the word of the Lord.
Thanks be to God.

☙❧

Philip, the angel and the eunuch

T he Gospel accounts provide plenty of comic moments,
but the Acts of the Apostles is also worth some attention. It contains some really big laughs, especially in
scenes that involve angelic encounters and divine intervention. These often play out comically. Equivalent scenes in
films would be hard to play entirely seriously because of the
comic juxtaposition of the shining angelic messenger next to
an apostle who had his own plans for the day.

The first curious incident I will mention – and thereby
ruin for you – can be found in chapter 8, where we find Philip
having a really weird day at the office.

Early manuscripts do not include the following
An angel of the Lord spoke to Philip, saying, 'Arise, and
go toward the south to the way that goes down from
Jerusalem to Gaza. This is a desert.'

'You're not exactly selling it,' said Philip.

'Okay, Philip,' said the angel. 'Less to say, more obey?
Chop chop.'

And so Philip went; and behold, there was a man of
Ethiopia, a eunuch of great authority under Candace,
queen of the Ethiopians, who had come to Jerusalem to
worship.

While there, the eunuch had attended a local sporting
fixture at which someone was holding up a sign. It said,
'Isaiah 3.16', and he wondered to himself what the sign
could mean.

Returning and sitting in his chariot, the eunuch was reading the prophet Isaiah, which is quite a big scroll to read in a very confined space. And as he went along, the papyrus did flap everywhere. Eventually, he found chapter 3 verses 16 and 17, which said:

Moreover Yahweh said, 'Because the daughters of Zion are arrogant,
    and walk with outstretched necks and flirting eyes,
    walking to trip as they go,
    jingling ornaments on their feet;
therefore the Lord brings sores on the crown of the head of the women of Zion,
    and Yahweh will make their scalps bald.'

'Wow,' said the eunuch. 'I was not expecting to find that in Isaiah.'

And the eunuch started scrolling through the rest of Isaiah to get the gist. But his eyes were not opened.

Then the Spirit said to Philip, 'Go near, and join yourself to this chariot.'

'Seriously?' said Philip. 'He's in a horse-drawn chariot. I'm just a guy on two legs.'

'Well, you'd better get a move on, then, hadn't you?' said the angel. 'Chop chop.'

'Stop saying that. Anyway, it's all right for you,' said Philip. 'You're an angel! You've got wings!'

'Do you see wings? I don't have wings. It's only cherubim and seraphim who have wings, and they are technically never called angels. Come on, Philip, you should know this. Anyway, that eunuch's getting away.'

So Philip ran to him, and as he ran, he heard him reading Isaiah the prophet.

Philip said, 'Do you understand what you are reading?'

He said, 'How can I, unless someone explains it to me?'

'Sure. The thing about Isaiah is that he's a prophet who . . . sorry, I've got a stitch,' said Philip, panting for breath.

And the eunuch pulled over and begged Philip to come up and sit with him. And Philip held his side and breathed heavily.

'I'll be all right in a minute,' said Philip.

'Make yourself comfortable in my chariot,' said the eunuch, pointing to a seat. 'Mind the cup holder.'

And they went on their way.

Now the passage of the Scripture that the eunuch had then turned to in Isaiah was this:

He was led as a sheep to the slaughter.
As a lamb before his shearer is silent,
so he doesn't open his mouth.
In his humiliation, his judgment was taken away.
Who will declare His generation?
For his life is taken from the earth.

The eunuch answered Philip, 'Who is the prophet talking about? About himself, or about someone else?'

And Philip wondered to himself, 'Is this an evangelistic opportunity? I mean, I don't want to push Jesus down his throat and come across as all "preachy".'

Then he saw the angel with his head in his hands,

muttering something about how even the mouths of donkeys had been opened by the Lord.

Then Philip opened his mouth, and beginning from this Scripture, preached to the eunuch about Jesus.

The eunuch then asked many more questions about Isaiah the prophet, for the scroll was long and hard to understand. And Philip said that, to be honest, Christians only really talk about the bits that are blatantly referring to Jesus and tend not to worry about the rest. And the eunuch found this puzzling given how long it is, and how you would want to listen to all the words of a prophet of God and how much of the Scriptures are taken up by the words of Isaiah the prophet so he must be important. And Philip said that he'd never really thought about it.

Then Philip said, 'So here's my question for you.'

'Is it about me being a eunuch?' said the eunuch.

'Erm,' said Philip. 'Would that be bad?'

But then the eunuch said, 'Behold, here is water. What is keeping me from being baptized?'

He commanded the chariot to stop, and they went down into the water, both Philip and the eunuch, and he baptized him. When they came up out of the water, the Spirit of the Lord caught Philip away, and the eunuch didn't see him any more, for he went on his way rejoicing, albeit puzzled.

But Philip was found at Azotus. And the angel said to him, 'There, you didn't expect that, did you?'

'No, I did not,' said Philip. 'Did I just dematerialize and reappear somewhere else?'

'Yup,' said the angel.

'But . . . how . . . what . . . why . . . is it . . . surely . . .' said Philip.

'Yes. Something like that,' said the angel. 'This might be the oddest moment in the whole Bible.'

'You mean I'm going to be famous?' said Philip.

'Not really,' said the angel. 'No one will read this bit. A bit like most of Isaiah.'

'Touché,' said Philip.

'And those who do read it will think it's so weird they won't really want to acknowledge it,' said the angel.

'Oh,' said Philip. 'Pity.'

'Yep,' said the angel. 'Back to work. Chop chop.'

And so passing through, Philip preached the good news to all the cities, until he came to Caesarea.

This is not the word of the Lord.
Thanks be to God.

℘℘

79

The truth will set you free

When Scripture is read out loud, most people aren't expecting to laugh. It turns out I'm not 'most people'. This was made publicly obvious a couple of years ago at an august meeting of the General Synod of the Church of England. During an act of worship at the end of a day's session, someone read aloud some Scripture. I think it was John 8. And it made me laugh out loud. I was the only person to laugh, naturally, and I felt like Sarah in Genesis 18 being told she would bear a son. Except I felt synodical, rather than divine, disapproval.[1]

I think I laughed at the bit where Nathanael laughs in this retelling, starting at John 8.31.

Jesus therefore said to those Jews who had believed him, 'If you remain in my word, then you are truly my disciples. You will know the truth, and the truth will make you free.'

They answered him, 'We are Abraham's offspring, and have never been in bondage to anyone. How do you say, "You will be made free"?'

Earlier manuscripts do not include the following
'Ha ha!' said Nathanael.

The Jews looked at Nathanael.

'Sorry, couldn't help overhearing,' said Nathanael. 'Funny you saying you've never been in bondage to

---

1 Synodical and divine approval are often not the same.

anyone. Classic. I'd high-five you but there are too many of you. Oh, what the heck.'

And Nathanael did put up his hand to high-five. And no one did high-five him.

'What do you mean?' said the Jews. 'We weren't kidding. We are Abraham's offspring, and have never been in bondage to anyone.'

'Nice. Never break character. Love the commitment,' said Nathanael.

'Seriously, we have no idea what you're talking about,' said the Jews.

'Wow,' said Nathanael. 'You mean you're not . . . Okay. I mean, us Jews saying we've never been in bondage or enslaved is like Romans saying, "We are Romans. We've never built roads, worn togas or used cruelty to animals as a form of entertainment." That's their thing. It's what they do. It's who they are!'

So the Jews said to him, 'Look, where are you going with this?'

'Hello?!' said Nathanael. '"We've never been in bondage to anyone"? You know the Passover? The biggest event of the year? What does that celebrate?'

'Fair enough. We often forget the true meaning of Passover,' said one of the Jews.

'It has become a bit commercialized,' said another. 'Did anyone see the Passover advert for Ehud's Emporium? Talk about oblique.'

'Yeah,' said another. 'These days, it's all, "Who's got the best hand-reared, most perfect organic lamb with the reddest blood?" We really need to get back to the basics of Passover.'

'But what was the point of the Passover, people?' said Nathanael.

There was a pause.

'To rel . . . e God's p . . . ple from slv . . . ry,' mumbled the Jews.

'To what?' said Nathanael.

'To release God's people from slavery,' muttered the Jews.

'Again?' said Nathanael.

'TO RELEASE GOD'S PEOPLE FROM SLAVERY! FROM BONDAGE! WE WERE SLAVES IN EGYPT FOR CENTURIES!' yelled the Jews. 'OKAY? HAPPY NOW?'

'And what happened after God's people took the land of Canaan? I'm thinking Judges?' said Nathanael. 'That's right, a continual cycle of doing evil in the sight of the Lord and being delivered into the hands of our enemies.'

Then Philip said, 'Nate? I think they get it. In fact, we were kind of enjoying the irony until you pointed it out.'

'Oh, so I'm the bad guy here?' said Nathanael. 'Look at them. They're literally looking around for rocks they can throw at Jesus.'

'No, Nate. I think those rocks might be for you,' said Philip.

'Oh. Tough crowd,' said Nathanael. 'Don't shoot the messenger.'

'We like shooting messengers,' said the crowd.

'It's okay,' said Philip. 'Nathanael didn't mean anything by what he was saying. Let's all just calm down.'

Then the Jews said, 'Can we get back to the truth setting us free? That sounded good.'

'Yes,' said Philip. 'And I'm sure Jesus is going to explain what he means and we can all just relax.'

Then Jesus said, 'Before Abraham was, I AM.'

'Told you!' cried the Jews. 'Get him! Grab those rocks!'

And there was a great commotion.

This is not the word of the Lord.
Thanks be to God.

☙❧

Another previously deleted parable

Or: Peter and the Parable of the Ten Bridesmaids

I love the film *Labyrinth*. I first saw it in 1987 and enjoyed showing it to my kids last year. One of my favourite parts is when Sarah (Jennifer Connelly) hits upon the idea of making marks on the ground to make sure she doesn't go round in circles. But when her back is turned, little goblins pick up the tiles she's marked and point them in a different direction. Sneaky.

This happens when I read the parables that Jesus tells. I sit and study a parable, working out what Jesus is clearly saying, only to return later to see that, suddenly, everything is pointing in a different direction. You notice a detail you could have sworn wasn't there before. You look back at the context of the parable, and it changes everything. There's a kicker that you've only just noticed.

I had this experience recently with the Parable of the Talents (Matthew 25.14–30). A man goes on a journey and gives three servants different amounts of money. A talent is about twenty years' wages for a labourer.[1] Shall we say half a million pounds in today's money? He gives one worker five talents, one two talents, and one only a single talent. I had

---

1 The New International Version translates the talent as a 'bag of gold'. Don't get me started on Bible translations.

assumed, being well educated and born in one of the wealthiest nations in the world, that I was the five talents guy.

At that moment, it dawned on me that maybe I wasn't the one with five talents. Or the one talent. But maybe I'm the guy with two talents. The one in the middle. Not a disaster. Not remarkable. Ordinary. Average. Below average, even. Maybe I'm, well, not as talented as I thought I was. This obviously says more about me than the parable, but maybe that's the point. Parables mess with your head, or at least hold up a mirror and show you things you've had stuck in your teeth all day that no one pointed out. And then I realized that's a feature of parables, not a bug.

Parabolical behaviour

What is the context for that Parable of the Talents? Just before is the Parable of the Ten Bridesmaids (Matthew 25.1–13). Or Virgins. It's a parable I've always struggled with because the characters don't quite do and say what you might think. And to make the parable work, potentially unchristian behaviour is commended. But maybe the wise bridesmaids did the right thing after all. You'll see what I mean in this alternative version I wrote and placed on the lips of my usual fall guy, Peter, during his Sending Out of The Seventy AD 28–29 Tour.

Early manuscripts do not include the following
Then Peter told them this parable:

'At that time the kingdom of heaven will be like ten bridesmaids who took their lamps and went out to meet the bridegroom. Five of them were wise and five were foolish – although they didn't know this at the time.

'The foolish ones took their lamps but did not take any oil with them, which was foolish.

'The wise ones, however, took oil in jars along with their lamps, which was wise.

'The bridegroom was a long time in coming, because weddings take ages.

'So the bridesmaids waited and there was a discussion about whether they were bridesmaids or virgins, but one bridesmaid was quite insistent that "bridesmaid" was a better translation than "virgin", so they stuck with that.

'When they realized they were discussing Bible translations, they became drowsy and fell asleep.

'At midnight, the cry rang out, "Here's the bridegroom! Come out to meet him!"

'Then all the bridesmaids woke up and trimmed their lamps. The foolish ones said to the wise, "Give us some of your oil; our lamps are going out."

'The wise ones replied, "No."

'"Please?" said the foolish ones.

'"No," replied the wise ones. "There may not be enough for both us and you."

'"Yeah, we get that. We were thinking that you might share?" said the foolish ones.

'"No," replied the wise ones.

'"That's not very Christian," said the foolish ones. "What happened to the Good Samaritan? Going the extra mile?"

'"It's more like the Parable of the Shrewd Manager," replied the wise ones.

'"Let's not go there," said the foolish ones.

'"If you want oil," said the wise bridesmaids, "go to those who sell oil and buy some for yourselves."

'"Brilliant idea. Go to those who sell oil. How do you think of these things? Wait a minute. It's midnight. Who's going to sell oil at midnight to a woman in first-century Judea?"

'"Not our problem," said the wise ones.

'"Unbelievable," said the foolish ones, as they left.

'But while the foolish ones were on their way to buy the oil, the bridegroom arrived.

'"What time do you call this?" said the wise ones.

'"All right, virgins?" said the bridegroom.

'"We're going with 'bridesmaids'?" they replied. "Anyway, it's past midnight. What on earth has been going on in there?"

'"Cut me some slack," said the bridegroom. "It's my wedding day. Do you have any idea how long it takes to get the wedding pictures done two thousand years before the camera is invented? I knew going with a sculptor was a mistake. We've been sat there for six hours and he's only just finished the bottom of my legs. Anyway, you must be starving. Come in."

'And so the bridesmaids who were ready went in with him to the wedding banquet. And the door was shut.

'Later the others also came. "Lord, Lord," they said, "open the door for us!"

'But the bridegroom replied, "Truly, I tell you, I don't know you."

'"Are you kidding me?" replied the bridesmaids. "We've been up all day and half the night and just had to schlep to a very dodgy service station on the other side of Jerusalem to buy oil. Open. This. Door. Now!"

'But he said again, "Truly, I tell you, I don't know you."

'"You don't know us? You invited us to your wedding. We're bridesmaids. Your insane wife chose these ridiculous dresses that make our arms look fat. And now we're freezing because it's gone midnight and someone won't let us go inside."

'"I can't," said the bridegroom. "It'll ruin the parable. Sorry, virgins. I mean, bridesmaids. Although I don't know why you don't want to be called virgins because . . . Oh, hello, Sally. Didn't know you were invited. Hashtag awkward."'

When he had finished saying these things, Peter turned to the disciple whom Jesus loved and said to him, 'There you go, John. You can have that!'

And John replied, 'You're all right, thanks.'

This is not the word of the Lord.
Thanks be to God.

☙❧

Pilgrim's Progress Part 2

Christian was still on his journey to the Celestial City. He had left Vanity Fair, walked past the Shops of Permanent Discounts and managed to avoid the Restaurant That Smells Amazing But You Just Can't Get Any Service.

Out on the open road, he came across a stream where he met three men who said their names were Contrarian, Wise After the Event and Breaking the Fourth Wall.[1]

'That's an interesting name,' said Christian to Contrarian.

'No, it isn't,' said Contrarian.

'Well, I think it is,' said Christian, trying to think of something else nice to say. 'In fact, being able to take up an adversarial position can be useful in defining the truth.'

'Not necessarily,' said Contrarian.

'I was trying to be nice,' said Christian. 'You're obviously quite a negative person.'

'No, I'm not,' said Contrarian.

'And I'm not sure that Contrarian is the best name for you, since you don't actually take up a contrary position, but merely disagree with anything I say.'

'No, I don't,' said Contrarian.

'I can't help feeling,' said Breaking the Fourth Wall, 'that this is going to end up being a predictable rip-off of the Monty Python Argument sketch.'

'No, it won't,' said Contrarian.

---

1 'Breaking the fourth wall' is when a character steps out of a play or show to address the audience directly.

Wise After the Event looked at Christian and smiled at him and said, 'Well, that pretty much went as expected.'

Christian felt sorry for these men, trapped by the personalities that they'd been handily labelled with since birth. Christian began to reason with them, inviting them to go with him to the Celestial City.

'I cannot go,' said Contrarian, 'not now you've invited me. It's in my nature to do the opposite of what you say.'

'I suppose he was bound to say that,' said Wise After the Event.

'And I know that you make it alone because I can skip forward to the end,' said Breaking the Fourth Wall.

'But surely there is nothing to stop you from coming with me?' said Christian.

'I cannot,' said Wise After the Event. 'I must remain to look after my family. I have three younger brothers: Saw You Coming, Slow Hand Clap and Crushing Sense of the Inevitable.'

'That is unfortunate,' said Christian.

'No, he lives next door,' said Wise After the Event.

'What?' said Christian.

'Unfortunate. That's the name of the man who lives next door,' said Wise After the Event. 'With his wife Ill-fated and their daughters Clumsy, Accident-prone and You'll Have Someone's Eye Out With That. I say they live next door. They keep having to move in with their mum as their house is always being burned to the ground.'

'Oh dear,' said Christian.

'Come on,' said Wise After the Event. 'You really should have seen that one coming.'

'Not really,' said Christian. 'I'm a Christian on my way to the Celestial City.'

'That is true,' said Wise After the Event. 'We had three people like you come through here the other day. What were they called? Oh, yes, Overly Sincere, Sense of Humour Failure, and There's No Need for Language.'

'So my attitude to you shouldn't be a surprise, should it?' said Christian. 'I'm surprised you didn't see that coming.'

'Touché,' said Wise After the Event.

Christian decided to move on.

Contrarian saw him look at the stream. 'To proceed on your way,' he said, 'you must step across the Stream of Unseen Perils. But it looks perfectly safe, if you ask me.'

Christian saw a stone in the middle of the stream, and wondered what this heavy-handed metaphor had in store for him. He stepped onto the stone in the middle of the stream, but it was covered in the Damp Moss of Doctrinal Imprecision. And Christian slipped and fell face first into the water.

Christian looked up at Wise After the Event and said to him, 'Not. One. Word.'

Contrarian, Wise After the Event and Breaking the Fourth Wall returned home.

'Not sure that was worth revisiting,' said Breaking the Fourth Wall.

'People like callbacks,' said Wise After the Event.

'I don't,' said Contrarian.

☙❧

Peter and the Sadducees

Being narcissists, we think we live in a uniquely argumentative age, with Twitter and trolling and passionate punditry. Look back in history and you'll see this is nothing new. As we've already seen, the likes of Bunyan were imprisoned for speaking out of turn. After the English Civil War, printing presses were heavily regulated to stop the war of pamphlets leading to more bloodshed. Nonetheless, the coffee houses of London became hotbeds of divided and vituperative opinion.

We shouldn't be surprised to find arguments in the Bible. In fact, an awful lot of the Gospel accounts are not parables, miracles and teaching, but blazing rows with religious leaders who quibbled over everything and attempted to entrap Jesus in his own words. In Luke 20, we read of one such attempt in which Sadducees, the wealthy ruling elite, tried to tie Jesus in knots over marriage after death. It's rather preposterous and silly. And so I imagined an even sillier version with Peter.

Earlier manuscripts do not include the following
One day the Sadducees came to Peter with a question.

'Teacher,' they said, 'Moses says that if a man dies without children, his brother must marry the widow and raise up offspring for him. Now imagine a family with seven brothers, and the oldest marries a woman—'

'Wait,' said Peter. 'Are you telling a parable? No offence, but I tell the parables round here.'

'It's not really a parable,' said the Sadducees. 'More of a hypothetical situation.'

'That's fine, then,' said Peter. 'Carry on.'

'Right,' said the Sadducees. 'Thank you.'

'Oh, hang on,' said Peter. 'Aren't you the ones who don't believe in the resurrection?'

'That's right,' said the Sadducees. 'We don't. And the way to remember is that we don't believe in the resurrection, which makes us sad, you see?'

The Sadducees laughed at their own joke.

Peter said, 'It's probably just easier to remember it.'

'Fair enough,' said the Sadducees. 'Now imagine a family with seven brothers, and the oldest marries a—'

'Wait,' said Peter.

'What is it now?' said the Sadducees.

'All you Sadducees are talking at the same time,' said Peter. 'It's pretty weird. Impressive, though. As far as talking in unison goes, you've nailed it. But can just one of you talk?'

'Okay,' said all the Sadducees.

'Shall I tell this one?' said one of the Sadducees.

'Fine,' said all the other Sadducees.

'Now imagine a family with seven brothers,' said the Sadducee. 'And the oldest marries a woman, and then dies, leaving no children.'

'This is a sad story,' said Peter.

'Wait,' said the Sadducee. 'It gets worse. The oldest brother left his wife to his brother. And the same thing happened to the second.'

'That is very sad. But it does happen,' said Peter.

'Look, this is going to take ages if you keep doing this,' said the Sadducee. 'There are seven brothers.'

'Sorry,' said Peter. 'It's just . . . I'm sad, you see. Ha ha.'

The Sadducee stared at him, and then went on, 'The same thing happened to the second brother, and the third, right on down to the seventh. And finally, the woman died. Now then, at the resurrection, the wife will be with the seven brothers. Do you not think that would make a fabulous musical?'

'You what?' said Peter.

'Wouldn't it be great?' said the Sadducee. 'A woman and her seven ex-husbands in the afterlife.'

'But you don't even believe in the afterlife!' said Peter.

'I would if it had show tunes. Come on, *Seven Bridegrooms for One Bride* has got Broadway written all over it! Which husband did she love the most? Should she go back to her first love, the first brother? Maybe she's got some dead sisters you could throw in.'

'Ooh, how about celebrity casting?' said another Sadducee. 'What about that woman who'd been married five times and met your mate Jesus at that well?'

'The Samaritan woman?' said Peter.

'Oh, is she? Scratch that. No Samaritans. I mean, I'd cast her, but we have to think of the box office and the shareholders.'

The Sadducees burst into song. And the chief priests and the teachers of the law began to dance. It was surprisingly well coordinated.

'Okay, stop,' said Peter. 'This is ridiculous.'

'All right,' said the Sadducees. 'The dance is a work in progress, but it's coming together.'

'No,' said Peter. 'I can't believe we've spent all this time building up to this absurd idea that the seven husbands story should be a musical. It's highly inappropriate. First, did not our Lord say that in heaven there will be no giving of each other in marriage?'

'Did he?' said the Sadducees. 'To be quite honest, we don't really listen to what that guy is saying.'

'Well, there's your first mistake,' said Peter. 'And second, you don't even believe in the resurrection. Your theology should not be affected by show tunes. And third, this whole idea about seven bridegrooms and one wife should obviously be a reality show. Or at the very least, some kind of *Mr and Mrs*. Call it *Mr and Mr and Mr and Mr and Mr and Mr and Mr and Mrs*.'

At that point, the Sadducees tore their clothes. 'If only we'd thought of that!' they said. And they plotted for a way to steal his format.

This is not the word of the Lord.
Thanks be to God.

CR EO

Rude interruptions

'You can't fight in here! This is the war room!'
President Merkin Muffley
Dr Strangelove or: How I learned to
stop worrying and love the bomb

Philip and the Ethiopian eunuch is a very strange passage of Scripture in many ways, but the sitcom writer in me is more drawn to the extraordinary account of Peter's miraculous release from prison in Acts 12. There's a moment reminiscent of that moment in *Dr Strangelove* when a fight breaks out in the war room, as quoted above. Here, a prayer meeting for Peter's miraculous release from jail is rudely interrupted by Peter banging at the door.

In this part of Acts, King Herod has just killed John's brother James. Realizing this was a vote-winner (despite being king), Herod has Peter thrown in jail. He is guarded by four squads of four soldiers, so no one is very optimistic about Peter's chances of escape. And so the early church holds a prayer vigil, which turns out to be surprisingly effective. Peter's time to die for the faith has not yet come. So here is the elongated, non-canonical version of the incident with Peter, the angel and a servant girl called Rhoda:

Early manuscripts do not include the following
Peter was sleeping between two soldiers, bound with two chains. Guards in front of the door kept the prison.

And with that many big blokes in such a tight, confined space, there was a bad smell.

And behold, an angel of the Lord stood by him, and a light shone in the cell. Peter continued to sleep.

'Peter! Stand up quickly,' said the angel.

'No, Mum,' said Peter. 'I have to eat all the marmalade.'

'What?' said the angel.

'But there's not enough toast. I need more toast.'

Realizing that Peter was still asleep, the angel struck him on the side and woke him up, saying, 'Stand up quickly!' His chains fell off his hands. The angel said to him, 'Get dressed and put on your sandals.' He did so. The angel said to him, 'Put on your cloak and follow me.' And he went out and followed him. Peter didn't know that what was being done by the angel was real. He thought he was still dreaming.

'Wait,' said Peter. 'Am I on my way to sit an exam I've not revised for, and when I turn over the paper, it's blank? And I pick up my pen and it turns into marshmallow?'

'No,' said the angel.

'Hang on,' said Peter. 'Any minute now, Mr Collins, my PE teacher, is going to turn up dressed as a ballerina. But at least he'll have all the marmalade that I need.'

'This is not a dream!' said the angel.

When they were past the first and the second guard, they came to the iron gate that leads into the city, which opened to them by itself.

'Cool,' said Peter.

They went out, and went down one street, and immediately the angel departed from him.

When Peter had come to himself, he said, 'Now I truly know that the Lord has sent out his angel and delivered me out of the hand of Herod, and from everything the Jewish people were expecting. And no sign of Mr Collins and the marmalade! Result!'

Simon who was called Peter came to the house of Mary – not that Mary – the mother of John who was called Mark, which is all very confusing when you're still half asleep. There many were gathered together, praying. When Peter knocked at the door of the gate, a servant girl named Rhoda came to answer.

'Hello?' said Peter.

'Peter? Is that really you?' said Rhoda with delight.

She recognized Peter's voice but she didn't open the gate for joy. Instead, she ran in and reported that Peter was standing in front of the gate.

'Yes, it's me! Er, hello?' said Peter. 'Fugitive on the run here, standing in the street, worried about guards with swords coming any minute!'

Rhoda said to those who had been praying, 'Peter is at the door!'

'Isn't it a gate?' said James. Not the James who was dead. This was another James.

'Not now,' said one of the elders, who hushed everyone, saying they were at prayer. But Rhoda was insistent.

They said to her, 'Look, there is no way Peter can be at the door! He's in jail, remember? We should know because we're praying for his release!'

'Can you hear what you're saying?' said Rhoda. 'Peter is at the door.'

'That will be his angel.'

'His angel? Who sounds exactly like Peter?' said Rhoda. 'Yeah, cos that's a thing.'

'There's no need to be like that,' they said. 'Anyway, if you're so sure it's Peter, why didn't you let him in?'

'That's a good point,' said Rhoda. 'I don't know.'

'May we remind you that we have received apostolic teaching so we should know that— sorry, there is an infernal knocking sound. Rhoda, make it go away.'

Rhoda went and opened the door and the gate, and they saw him and were amazed.

Peter said, 'Tell these things to James and to the brothers. And that I was standing here for ages and you didn't let me in!'

'Why don't you come in?' they said. But he departed and went to another place.

This is not the word of the Lord.
Thanks be to God.

CR ℰᴏ

Christians according
to sitcom writers

If you're a Christian and you see Christians portrayed in TV sitcom or drama, you brace yourself. You're going to cringe. You're probably not expecting to be skewered for hypocrisy. You're more likely to be represented as being weird or out of touch. Imagine a sitcom scene in which the hero is invited to a Bible study. What are the other people at the Bible study like in this scene? Exactly.

Where did this start? It would be tempting to point the finger at *Monty Python's Life of Brian*. It's a brilliant film. Mostly. I have a couple of issues with the ending, but multiple interviews and retrospectives have made it clear that the goal of the angry young Pythons was not Jesus, or even Christianity, but Religion.

Nonetheless, many religious people resented it deeply, hated the idea of it and didn't see it. For them, the thought of some young over-educated punks slagging off their Saviour wasn't worth their time, money or attention. Fair enough. They could be forgiven for thinking that and deciding against seeing the film.

For some, perhaps there was a suspicion that the edifice of Christianity in our nation might prove to have feet of clay, being unable to withstand an attack from the cool kids. For others, they did not appreciate Python-esque silliness being found anywhere near sacred matters.

This was all back in 1979. I was only four years old. But the way things are now goes back further than Monty Python, to the early 1960s. That was when the post-war world of deference was comically and cartoonishly kicked to death. The Angry Young Men joined forces with the devastatingly funny, albeit slightly less angry, men from *Beyond the Fringe*. Alan Bennett's mockery of bland, vapid sermons and Peter Cook's impersonations of the Prime Minister showed a contempt for the versions of Church and State that were on offer at the time. This in turn saw the fringe and nightclub-style cabaret move centre stage on television through *That Was the Week That Was*, *Not So Much a Programme, More A Way of Life* and *BBC3*. Then came *The Frost Report*, which was broadcast on BBC1 in 1966.

All Gas and Gaiters

This would suggest the 1966 sitcom *All Gas and Gaiters* was never going to last long. The show centred on a bishop, his chaplain, the archdeacon and the dean of the cathedral. Even at the time, it must have seemed like the hangover from another era, which featured Christians essentially bickering over dwindling power. It's quite possible that even then, Anglicans had little understanding of the differences between domains of bishops and deans.

And so Christianity, little by little, has been edged off our screens, albeit more slowly from our radios.[1] To its credit, BBC Radio 4 still broadcasts a daily church service, but

---

1 As if to demonstrate this, *All Gas and Gaiters* ran on television until 1971, whereupon it was immediately re-recorded for radio. This, however, was common practice at the time, and numerous TV shows, including *Dad's Army*, *To the Manor Born* and *Yes Minister*, were all re-recorded for radio.

you won't find much on any other BBC Radio channels.[2] This trend isn't just true of BBC television, but also of ITV, Channel 4 and Channel 5, some of whom commission the occasional documentary which sensationally says all over again what German Liberal Protestant theologians were saying a hundred years ago, that whatever the Bible says happened at a particular place, probably didn't. Flick over to channels that proport to broadcast history programmes and you'll find hours of documentaries about Bible codes, holy bloodlines and Vatican conspiracy theories.

All the above means that when Christianity is represented on mainstream television, it's standing for an awful lot of Christian diversity and a large range of views. But at that point, the most important thing is the audience's preconceptions of what Christians are like. Do writers want to reinforce stereotypes and play with them? Or subvert them?

Christians in sitcoms

Few writers working in the UK today have any great desire to challenge the way the Great British people think about Christianity. So those of us who are both Christians and sitcom writers[3] are often asked why we can't write a sitcom in which Christianity is represented in a fair and reasonable light, rather than being a fringe issue. We can't. And there are a couple of reasons for this.

---

2 A short while back, I pitched some audio religious programmes for alternatives to BBC Radio 4, but was told that religion was 'niche'. It's worth thinking about how humanity's greatest primeval desire to worship and know our creator, in all cultures and throughout history, is now 'niche'.

3 We occasionally meet up in a very small room above a pub in London. There aren't many of us.

Given how times have changed, TV commissioners aren't currently interested in representing the Christian faith favourably, or at all. It's not their job. They just want comedy and drama. Anything that feels too partisan or hard to identify with won't get very far.

Defining characters

It's also difficult to put Christian characters in 'regular' situations without their faith completely defining them. Sitcom characters tend to be larger than life and have a main characteristic, otherwise things get confusing. And, as I often say on my *Sitcom Geeks* podcast, 'confusion is the enemy of comedy'. You must keep things simple. So if your character is a Christian, like Mary in Peter Kay's *Phoenix Nights*, she's going to be defined by her faith and not appear 'normal'. Hence her nickname in the show: 'Holy Mary'. The faith will always unbalance and come to define the character.

There's also an issue here that Christians need to get their heads around, those who might want to say their faith doesn't define them. But if you're a Christian, your faith does define you. My faith defines me. Through Christ I am a child of God. Read any of the Gospels and you'll see that faith in Christ is seen as the defining issue, transcending race, gender and class.

Even so

The realities of all the above are frustrating, however, when you so rarely see your faith reflected on TV, especially when you see Christians, vicars, priests or nuns do or say things you know they would just never do. There may have been some truth in them many years ago, but these are very old stereotypes that won't go away. I'm sure doctors feel the same watching medical dramas and police feel the same watching cop shows, counting off incorrect terminology and shortcuts that are now sackable offences.[4]

So, given I'm not going to resurrect *All Gas and Gaiters*, or have my own sitcom about real-life Christians as they are today, I can at least help get Christians represented more accurately in existing sitcoms, detective shows and dramas, rather than relying on third-hand stereotypes from the television of yesteryear.[5]

And so I've produced a handy guide for any sitcom or drama writers reading this book. Please tear the page along the dotted line and place near your writing desk for easy reference.

* * *

Here are some things that Christians don't really do or haven't really done for decades in the UK, so would you be so kind as to remove them from your scripts? Many thanks.

---

4 Having written a show set in the army, *Bluestone 42*, I know the pain of trying to get the details right, which normally makes things better and feel more real. Sometimes, though, it is just confusing and so you have to make compromises. And sometimes you're shooting a scene on the fly, you've about 14 minutes left before the light goes and you have to start paying overtime, so occasionally you have to take the path of least resistance. It pleases me greatly, however, that I still get compliments from soldiers who say that, of all the TV shows they've seen on army life, ours is closest to what it's actually like.

5 There are some fun explanations of Christian and religious stereotypes at <tvtropes.org>. See 'Token Religious Teammate' and 'Church of St Genericus'. There are lots of examples in 'TV and Movies' if you scroll to the bottom of the page.

1 We don't sing 'Kumbaya'

If you want to portray Christians gathering at a demonstration or protest, you might be tempted to have them start to sing 'Kumbaya' as some kind of Christian protest song. They wouldn't. Christians don't sing it any more. And if they did, they would be self-consciously giggling at the insufferable naffness of it. It would, in itself, be a joke. In the 1970s and 1980s, some Christians did sing it without irony. Fine. It's a fair cop. If your show is set in the 1970s, go ahead. But even by the 1990s, the song was a bit of a joke. Now it's not even retro. In the 1990s, we were singing 'Shine, Jesus, Shine' by Graham Kendrick (or some of us were anyway).

I have broken this rule myself, but explaining why might be helpful. In an episode of *Another Case of Milton Jones* for BBC Radio 4 that I co-wrote,[6] there is a joke about ancient Rome and the idea of someone screaming defiantly that they don't want to be thrown to the Christians. The joke, clearly, is that this would be even worse than being thrown to the lions. At that point, the cast start singing 'Kumbaya'. When writing radio, you have to grab the most easily identifiable sound or word, since you don't have any visuals to land the joke. It just felt right that the Christians would be singing 'Kumbaya' and that this, for the criminal, would be a fate worse than death. But the *Milton Jones* world is very cartoonish, so there is no pretence that Christians really sing that song any more.[7]

---

6 I co-wrote *Another Case of Milton Jones* with Milton who is also a Christian. I think he came up with this joke, but I was more than happy to go along with it, as it just works.

7 For more on joke mechanics and stereotypes, see Part 1 of *The Sacred Art of Joking*.

2 We don't sing 'All Things Bright and Beautiful'

If you're setting a scene at a regular Anglican church service, there's very little chance they will be singing 'All Things Bright and Beautiful', as they might have done at your primary school back in the 1970s. If your show is set in the 2020s and your protagonist enters the church during a service and sits down at the back, trying to 'blend in' during the hymn, they will not be singing this hymn.

Don't get me wrong. This old hymn has its upsides, being a simple song of gratitude for God's creation, but it has fallen out of favour and the people who enjoyed singing it have long since passed away, or become sufficiently elderly that their views are now unreasonably excluded.

If you're looking for alternative hymns, I need to issue some words of warning. A BBC *Songs of Praise* poll might show up when you Google 'hymns'. This shows that Britain's favourite him is 'Jerusalem'.[8] All that really tells you is who votes in BBC *Songs of Praise* polls. Singing 'Jerusalem' may make people feel good, partly because the tune is brilliant and it causes a swell of national pride, but the congregation in your script almost certainly won't be singing it. The vicar probably wouldn't allow it, given it's far too jingoistic and it's not really got much to do with the Christian faith. The same goes for 'I Vow to Thee My Country' (number 6 in the poll), which is for posh people who like rugby.[9]

---

8 'Jerusalem revealed as the UK's favourite hymn on BBC Songs of Praise special', BBC Media Centre, 29 September 2019, <https://bbc.co.uk/mediacentre/latestnews/2019/songs-of-praise-favourite-hymn> (accessed 27 January 2021).

9 I probably fit into that category.

So may I recommend 'Be Thou My Vision' to the lilting tune of 'Slane', 'How Great Thou Art', 'Amazing Grace' or 'When I Survey the Wondrous Cross'?

The only exception to all the above is if the church service is a funeral – and the person being buried didn't go to church. In that case, 'All things Bright and Beautiful' is quite a popular choice. It's often chosen by people who don't know any hymns because they don't go to church, and because they see people sing the hymn on TV and so assume that churchgoers still sing it. The result is a whole church of people singing a hymn that no one really wants to be singing. Which is quite funny. But annoying.[10]

3 We don't refer to the Bible as 'The Good Book'

We just don't. We call it the Bible. Because it is.[11]

4 We tend not to kneel down to pray

Some do in Church of England churches, on those old kneelers. But the vast majority of people who are in the habit of doing that probably shouldn't and might have problems getting up again.

---

10 I would have included 'The Lord of the Dance' song on my list of songs Christians no longer sing, but during a meeting of the local deanery synod just before Easter 2019, I was invited to sing this truly idiotic song without irony. It's hard to sing, 'It's hard to dance with the Devil on your back,' without laughing at the sheer artless absurdity of the lyrics. King David danced, but to describe Jesus as the 'Lord of the Dance' is, well, quite a leap.

11 It's always struck me as funny that when coming up with a TV series that has lots of episodes, and you're trying to create a document that tells other writers and producers about the world, the characters, the rules and the settings, you call that document a 'bible'. If you hear someone on TV talk about bibles, it'll be that kind. Not a Bible. Or The Bible. But a bible.

5 We don't generally refer to God as 'The Man Upstairs'

We don't – and also referring to God as a 'man' seems weird, or sexist, even though Jesus was (and is) a man.

6 Inviting the vicar for tea isn't really a thing

If the vicar comes round, we'll whack the kettle on, obviously. We're British. It's something to do and we all like tea. But it's not a tea party. No one's really panicking that everything needs to be perfect for the vicar. As we have seen in recent chapters, the status of the parish priest has changed in the established church. Perhaps people ran around frantically preparing for the vicar's arrival in the 1970s, during an episode of *Terry and June*, but *The Vicar of Dibley* probably put the Scary Important Vicar stereotype to bed, and then held a pillow over its face.

7 We don't say, 'The Lord moves in mysterious ways'

Okay, maybe we do, but we say it less often than you might think, and only when we can't think of anything else to say.

8 We aren't shocked and confused when someone asks us how a good God can allow suffering in the world AS IF NO ONE'S EVER MENTIONED THAT BEFORE

Apologies for raising my caps there, but this area troubled me so much that I wrote a play about it called *The God Particle*. In short, the secular media tends to show Christians as having a shallow understanding of their own faith. This is true in some cases, but we see it with tedious regularity in soaps and dramas. If you see a priest as a regular character, pretty soon something bad's going to happen to make that character doubt his or her Christian faith for the first time.[12]

Many Christians do doubt their faith, some a little, some a lot. But Christians have been thinking about suffering for two thousand years so it's unlikely this is really going to throw all of us for a loop.

9 We don't say things like, 'Jesus loves you'

We actually don't bang on about Jesus. We probably should, but mostly we don't.[13]

∽∾

---

12 In *Bluestone 42* we have a padre, and I was determined that one storyline we would not do was the padre having a crisis of faith because of the suffering in Afghanistan and the IEDs.

13 Partly as a result of this, a few years ago I made a conscious effort to change my 'See you later' or 'Take care' to 'God bless'.

Raising Lazarus

Lazarus returning from the dead takes Jesus' powers from stunning (feeding the five thousand) through eye-popping (walking on water) to off the charts. John tells the story in his Gospel. It is a familiar one, so it's easy to forget about the reactions of the regular folk, who probably included our friend Nathanael and perhaps Nicodemus. And so here is an unauthorized version of John 11.

Jesus therefore, again groaning in himself, came to the tomb. Now it was a cave, and a stone lay against it. Jesus said, 'Take away the stone.'

Martha, the sister of him who was dead, said to him, 'Lord, by this time there is a stench, for he has been dead four days.'

Earlier manuscripts do not include some of the following

'Way to kill the moment, Martha!' said Nathanael. 'Jesus was about to do a huge reveal there, and you come in with, "It's going to stink"!'

'Well, it is,' said Martha. 'You think I want to smell the stench of my brother's corpse?'

'Jesus is about to do something dramatic,' said Nathanael.

'Seriously, Nate?' said Philip. 'This is how you talk to a woman who is grieving her brother? Her dead brother. Man, read the room.'

'We're outside,' said Nathanael.

'Why are you still talking?' said Philip. 'Sorry, Martha. Sorry, Jesus. Do go on.'

Jesus said to her, 'Didn't I tell you that if you believed, you would see God's glory?'

So they took away the stone from the place where the dead man was lying. Jesus lifted up his eyes, and he cried with a loud voice, 'Lazarus, come out!'

'Er, question?' said Nathanael.

'This had better be good,' said Philip.

'Lazarus is completely bound up in bandages,' said Nathanael. 'He will literally not be able to move – or see, if there's a bandage over his eyes. If he's alive.'

'Now who's killing the moment?' said Philip.

'We're totally on the same scroll, here, Phil,' said Nathanael. 'Singing from the same psalm-sheet. I want that big moment too, but right now the most likely scenario is Lazarus trying to crawl out of the tomb like a wiggly worm.'

'Yeah, because Jesus hasn't given that any thought, being the SUPREME BEING who is OUTSIDE TIME, who can also raise people from the dead!'

'Can he, though?'

'Yes! He can! Look, there's Lazarus. And you ruined the moment. Well done, Nate.'

He who was dead came out, bound hand and foot with wrappings, and his face was wrapped around with a cloth.

Jesus said to them, 'Free him, and let him go.'

Therefore, many of the Jews who came to Mary and saw what Jesus did believed in him. But some of them went away to the Pharisees and told them the things which Jesus had done. The chief priests therefore and the Pharisees gathered a council, and said, 'What are we doing? For this man does many signs. If we leave him alone like this, everyone will believe in him.'

'Is that such a bad thing?' came a voice. 'I mean, if he's actually raising people from the dead, then shouldn't we, erm, believe in him too?'

The chief priests and the Pharisees turned and looked. They saw Nicodemus.

'Might have known it would be you, Nicodemus,' said Caiaphas. 'How's that being born again going for you?'

'Apparently, your mate Jesus is older than Abraham?' said one voice.

'And he says he's a good shepherd!' said another. 'But how can he be? He has literally zero track record of shepherding. We all know he's the son of a carpenter from Nazareth.'

And Caiaphas said, 'Ha! Nazareth! Can anything good come from Nazareth? Am I right? High-five?'

And one of the chief priests gave him a high-five.

'And don't get me started on Samaritans,' said Caiaphas.

'I heard Jesus was going to marry some Samaritan woman,' said another. 'That is not going to play with the crowds.'

'We've been through this!' said Nicodemus. 'He is the promised Messiah!'

'Nope,' said Caiaphas. 'To be the promised Messiah he would have to have been born in the City of David. That would be Bethlehem.'

'I THINK I KNOW THAT BETHLEHEM IS THE CITY OF DAVID!' roared Nicodemus.

And everyone said, 'Ooh, temper, temper.'

'But maybe he was born in Bethlehem. Wasn't there a census around the time he was born?' said Nicodemus.

'You just don't get it, do you?' said Caiaphas. 'If we let him go on like this, everyone will believe in him and the Romans will come and take away both our place and our nation.'

And Caiaphas said to them, 'You know nothing at all, nor do you consider that it is advantageous for us that one man should die for the people, and that the whole nation not perish.' So from that day forward they took counsel that they might put him to death.

Nicodemus laughed. 'Put him to death!' he said. 'Pull the other one. It's got leprosy!'

Caiaphas said, 'Nicodemus, please refrain from referring to unclean diseases. It's unseemly.'

'Says the high priest planning a murder,' said Nicodemus. 'Not that you'll succeed.'

'Why not?'

'Can't you hear what you've just said? You're basically saying, "This Jesus has power over life and death. Let's kill him!" It's not going to work. Duh.'

'It might,' said Caiaphas.

'I honestly don't think it will,' said Nicodemus.

'You don't know that!' yelled Caiaphas.

'Temper, temper,' said Nicodemus. 'Put it this way. If you manage to kill him, I'll personally put 75 pounds of myrrh and aloes on the dead body myself. Deal?'

'Wow, that's specific,' said Caiaphas. 'But, er, deal!'

Most of this is not the word of the Lord.
Thanks be to God.

The chief priests knew Jesus had the power to raise people from the dead, but assumed that killing Jesus wouldn't be a problem. But the disciples had the opposite view. When Jesus predicted his own death, his followers simply couldn't come to terms with what he was talking about. To them it was obvious that Jesus could not be killed. So maybe this bit was left out of Mark's Gospel:

Mark 10.32b–34 (more or less)

Jesus again took the twelve and began to tell them the things that were going to happen to him. 'Behold, the Son of Man will be delivered to the chief priests and the scribes. They will condemn him to death, and will deliver him to the Gentiles. They will mock him, spit on him, scourge him, and kill him. On the third day he will rise again.'

'Huh?' said Peter.

'What?' said Andrew.

'What's Jesus talking about?' said Peter.

'I have literally no idea,' said Andrew. 'Last one to Capernaum's a rotten egg!'

'I hate races! And you've got a head start! Come back! Not fair.'

CRεO

Peter and John are definitely not racing to the tomb. Honest

Therefore Peter and the other disciple went out, and they went toward the tomb. They both ran together. The other disciple outran Peter, and came to the tomb first.
John 20.3–4

This race to the tomb is one of the most puzzling parts of John's Gospel. Peter and John are running to the tomb in chapter 20, and once you see the competitiveness in the account, you can't unsee it. To make it clearer and funnier, I wrote a monologue which I perform in the style of a Bob Newhart telephone conversation where the audience only gets to hear one side of it. I play Peter calling John about this Gospel, and this chapter is that monologue.

[*Performed in the style of a Bob Newhart monologue*]

[PETER *gets out his telephone and phones* JOHN.]

Hi, John. Yes, Peter . . . just running through the proofs of your Gospel before it's out . . . Yeah, I do like it. Yeah. It's . . . great. Not like the other ones at all, really. Which is a good thing. Who wants more of the same?

Yep, I did read the new opening . . . Yep. 'In the beginning was the Word' . . . Sure. Why not? Who needs wise men or shepherds when you could . . . baffle people for

2,000 years with that? No, no . . . It's . . . well, it is what it is.

Look, the main reason for the call is the resurrection bit when Mary comes back to get us. Yeah, that bit seems to be missing from my . . . [*shuffles paper*] Do you know what? It's here. Sorry. It was stuck to the other one . . . No. It's fine, I'll just skim it now . . .

'Now on the first day of the week, Mary Magdalene went early, while it was still dark, to the tomb, and saw the stone taken away from the tomb. Therefore she ran and came to Simon Peter and to the other disciple . . .'

Who is that? Is that . . . oh, you go on to say, 'The one whom Jesus loved . . . And that's you, is it? . . . Right. He kind of loves everyone, doesn't he? . . . It just seems an odd way of talking about yourself, but hey, it's your Gospel.

'Therefore Peter and the other disciple went out, and they went toward the tomb. They both ran together. The other disciple outran Peter, and came to the tomb first.'

So, you're putting that in, are you? . . .

Well, wasn't really a race, was it? . . .

Okay, well, I didn't know we were racing . . . And I seem to remember you had a head start because you were nearer the door and . . . doesn't matter. I just think it's a strange detail to throw in but . . . okay. Forget it. We move on.

'Stooping and looking in, he saw the linen cloths lying, yet he didn't enter in. Then Simon Peter came, following him—'

Again, John, I think you've made it clear you got there first, so this just . . . no, I just . . . technically you are right. This is a true and correct record but I just . . . okay, fine . . .

'Then Simon Peter came, following him, and entered into the tomb. He saw the linen cloths lying, and the cloth that had been on his head, blah blah blah. So then the other disciple who came first to the tomb . . .'

John. Look. This is pretty weird . . . Okay? . . . You've taken the critical passage in the resurrection narrative of the Lord Jesus Christ, the single greatest event in human history, and used it to tell people that Jesus loved you the most and that you can run faster than me . . . when it wasn't even a race . . .

Yeah? Well . . . okay . . . fine. Take out the reference to a victory dance, and we'll say no more about it. Okay, bye.

CR&O

Paul, Silas and the jailer

Did Peter's escape from prison in Acts 12 set a pattern for the future? Maybe Silas thought so when he found himself imprisoned with Paul following an incident in Philippi (Acts 16). Here's how it could have gone:

Earlier manuscripts of Acts do not include some of the following

At about midnight Paul and Silas were praying and singing hymns to God, and the prisoners were listening to them. Some prisoners were none too thrilled about being exposed to modern worship songs and cried out for deliverance.

Suddenly there was a great earthquake, so that the foundations of the prison were shaken; and immediately all the doors were opened, and everyone's bonds were loosened. The jailer, being roused out of sleep and seeing the prison doors open, drew his sword and was about to kill himself, supposing that the prisoners had escaped. But Paul cried with a loud voice, saying, 'Don't harm yourself, for we are all here!'

'Speak for yourself, Paul,' said Silas, heading for the door.

'Whoa, whoa, whoa,' said Paul. 'Where do you think you're going?'

'Out? Away?' said Silas. 'Sorry, why do I need to explain this?'

'You stay right where you are, young man,' said Paul.

And Silas stood right where he was, for he was a young man.

'But there's been an earthquake. And we're all free,' said Silas. 'Just like Peter when he was delivered by that angel four chapters ago.'

Paul looked around. 'Well, I don't see any angels around here.'

'Seriously? There was an earthquake.'

'It might have been caused by your singing,' shouted one of the prisoners. 'No offence.'

'Okay, I'm no baritone,' said Paul. 'But we must give thanks to God at all times and in all places who has given us all things in Christ Jesus in whom we have every spiritual blessing . . .'

'And who sets the captives free,' said Silas. 'We're captives. Now we're free. Come on!'

'That's not meant to be taken literally,' said Paul.

'How can you say that?' said Silas. 'God literally set his people free in Egypt. With an earthquake. Wasn't that one of the plagues?'

'There were frogs, locusts and gnats,' said one of the prisoners.

'There was that weird one with the Nile turning to blood,' said another.

'There wasn't an earthquake!' said Paul. 'There was the water to blood, frogs, gnats, flies, pestilence, boils, hail . . . did I already say locusts? Silas? Silas!'

Silas was almost out of the door when the jailer called for lights, sprang in and fell down trembling before Paul and Silas. He brought them out, and said, 'Sirs, what must I do to be saved?'

'Let us go free,' said Silas.

'Be quiet, Silas!' said Paul. 'Believe in the Lord Jesus Christ, and you will be saved, you and your household.'

And they spoke the word of the Lord to him, and to all who were in his house. He took them the same hour of the night and washed their stripes, and was immediately baptized, he and all his household.

'So we baptize infants now?' said Silas.

'Let's not get into this,' said Paul. 'Just enjoy the moment.'

'Okay,' said Silas. 'As long as you categorically promise to cover it in one of your letters or something. I mean, it would be really annoying if Christians who are united over so many aspects of the gospel should fall out over baptism.'

'That would be a shame,' said Paul. 'Tell you what. I need to write another letter to the Romans. I'll put it in that.'

'Deal,' said Silas.

And when it was day, the magistrates sent the sergeants, saying, 'Let those men go.'

This is not the word of the Lord.
Thanks be to God.

൭൫൭

An angel in *A Christmas Carol*

London, 1843. The bedroom of Charles Dickens

Charles Dickens lay in bed, fast asleep. Although he was in debt and his latest novel had sold poorly, he was sleeping deeply, for he had just finished a new work that he felt could reverse his fortunes. The book was called *A Christmas Carol* and concerned a miserly figure called Ebenezer Scrooge.

As the clock struck one, the curtain rustled. The dog, sleeping by the glowing embers of the fire downstairs, woke up and then quickly dozed off again, unaware that in his master's bedroom, a shining white figure had appeared at the foot of the bed.

'Charles Dickens,' said the angel Gabriel.

Dickens did not respond.

'Charles Dickens,' repeated the angel Gabriel, a little louder but not loud enough to wake Mrs Dickens. But then again, it probably wasn't loud enough to wake Mr Dickens. He sighed to himself and said, 'This is Acts 12 all over again. I hope he doesn't sleep as deeply as the Apostle Peter.'

So he walked over to Charles's side of the bed and gave his side a shove. Charles Dickens opened his eyes and was afraid. He sat up in bed and stared in wonder at the archangel.

'Are you a spirit come to torment me?' said Charles Dickens.

'Do I look like a spirit?' said Gabriel.

'You mean, you're an angel?' said Dickens.

'An archangel, actually,' said Gabriel. 'You'd think that

would mean I don't have to run errands like this, but apparently not. Anyway, I've just come to kick the tyres on this book you've written because it feels like it is going to define Christmas for the English-speaking world for decades to come.'

'You mean *A Christmas Carol* is going to be a bestseller?' said Dickens with great excitement. 'Not that I wrote it in order to make money.'

The angel looked at the author, who looked away.

'Okay, I was hoping to clear a few bills,' said Dickens. 'Can you blame me? My last novel was not a success.'

'Who'd've thought no one wants to read a book called *Martin Chuzzlewit*?' said the angel. 'Where do you get these ridiculous names?'

'A friend of mine helps me think them up,' said Dickens. 'He is a delightful fellow by the name of Buckfast Nazalthrash.'

'I honestly can't tell if you're joking,' said Gabriel.

'Well, I've paid the price. I've fallen on hard times. Really hard times. Dire straits! Ooh, hang on.'

Dickens grabbed a quill and a scrap of paper and wrote, 'A novel called *Dire Straits*?'

'Here's the problem,' said the angel. 'Your book's great. Nice, simple three-act structure in the middle with ghosts of past, present and future. Three works for us in the heavenly realms for obvious reasons. It's just the beginning and the end we have some notes on.'

'Oh,' said the author. 'Please, if the work can be improved, I'm open to suggestions and corrections.'

'Really? Writers tend to hate notes,' said the angel. 'You should have seen the pushback when I visited Jude writing that letter for the New Testament. I suggested taking out the stuff about angels arguing over the body of Moses. It wasn't something Michael particularly wanted remembered but Jude was determined to keep it in, so I just left it.'

'Well, I like to think I can always improve on my craft and that my best work is yet to come,' said Dickens, eyeing his piece of paper that said, 'A novel called *Dire Straits*?'

The angel saw the note and said, 'Call it *Hard Times*. Not *Dire Straits*. Trust me.'

'Really? I can see *Dire Straits* being a global phenomenon,' said Dickens.

'So can I,' said the angel. 'Just not for you. Anyway, the beginning of your novel has a visit from Scrooge's old business partner, Marley. Do we need that?'

'What's wrong with it?' said Dickens.

'People speaking from beyond the grave? Do we want to encourage this sort of thing?' said the angel. 'I mean, these Victorians will need very little encouragement when it comes to seances and spiritualism.'

'You get it in the Bible,' said Dickens. 'One Samuel chapter 28? King Saul wants to talk to Samuel. Who is dead. So he goes to the Witch of Endor. And Samuel is actually summoned from the dead. Can you imagine? Saul, King of Israel, wants to hear the voice of Yahweh's prophet whom he ignored when he was alive. And in order to speak to him now he's dead, he has to use witchcraft, which should incur a death penalty!'

'That is quite funny,' said the angel. 'Never thought of it like that. Okay, Marley stays. But here's the other thing: the ending. The lesson that Scrooge learns feels like moralism. He's decided to be good. Do we really want to turn Christmas into a festival of non-specific, deistic Dickensfest?'

'It's just a made-up story,' said Dickens.

'Yeah, but you don't just become a good guy overnight without supernatural intervention,' said the angel.

'He sees four ghosts! How much supernatural intervention do you want?' said Dickens.

'I'm talking about the indwelling of the Holy Spirit,' said Gabriel.

'Yes, I realize that,' said Dickens. 'But this is a parable.'

'Sure,' said the angel. 'But the metaphorical and allegorical are tricky lines to walk, and—'

'No, no. It is literally a parable,' said Dickens. 'That Jesus tells?'

'Erm, I think I missed the Parable of the Four Ghosts and the Terrible Night's Sleep,' said the angel. 'Are you sure that's not the Gospel of Thomas?'

'Well, this is awkward,' said Dickens. 'Far be it from me to tell you what our Lord said, but the Parable of the Rich Man and Lazarus?'

'Go on,' said the angel.

'It's a parable Jesus tells in Luke's Gospel to the Pharisees "who loved money",' said Dickens. 'A rich man lives in luxury while a beggar called Lazarus lives at his gate. And when the beggar dies, he is carried up to heaven by angels. Do angels actually do that?'

'Some do,' said the angel. 'I don't. Being an archangel I take a more supervisory capacity. Annunciate saviours to virgins. That sort of thing.'

'Anyway, in the parable, the rich man dies, and is buried,' said Dickens. 'In Hades, he lifts up his eyes, being in torment, and sees Abraham far off, and who's right there with him?'

'Moses? Elijah?' said the angel. 'Wait, Enoch! People were very weird about him in Jesus' day.'

'No! Lazarus!' cried Dickens. 'There in heaven is the great Abraham with lowly pauper Lazarus.'

'That's just like Abraham. Very good with newcomers. Knows how to break the ice,' said the angel. 'I can never think of anything to say, and just stand there in bright raiment and people get terrified, but Abraham's able to put people at their ease. Although if he introduces you to his sister, you might wanna check that.'

'Yes, of course,' said Dickens. 'Anyway, the rich man cries out, but Abraham isn't having any of it and says the rich man had his chance. So the rich man says that Lazarus should be sent to warn his relatives so they won't be in the place of torment.'

'Isn't it incredible that the rich man is still bossing around poor Lazarus like a slave?' said the angel.

'Yes, I suppose it is,' said Dickens. 'But Abraham says they have Moses and the prophets. And the rich man says that if someone from the dead warns them, they will repent. But Abraham says that if they don't listen to Moses and the prophets, they won't listen to someone who has risen from the dead.'

'Ooh! Ooh! I get it. That's J— Wait. I should annunciate this properly,' said the angel, who drew himself up to his full height and was terrifying. The dog had picked the wrong moment to walk in on his master and ran back down the stairs. 'Behold, the one of whom you speak is Jesus Christ, son of David, Emmanuel.'

'Nicely done,' said Dickens. 'But this is how *A Christmas Carol* works: someone comes back from the dead to warn Scrooge to change his ways. And it works.'

'But Abraham said it wouldn't work,' said the angel.

'It's Christmas! That would be a bit of a downer for people reading at bedtime,' said Dickens. 'And so Scrooge wouldn't listen, died and went to Hades where he was tortured in burning agony for eternity. Goodnight, kids. Merry Christmas. Hope you haven't been naughty!'

'I take the point,' said the angel. 'It's probably fine, then. But I tell you what. I never had this trouble with John Bunyan. Say what you like about *Pilgrim's Progress*. No one is ever in any doubt about who represents what.'

'John Bunyan was a Puritan,' said Dickens. 'He probably believed that celebrating Christmas was sinful anyway.'

'You're probably right there,' said the angel. 'Mind you, Christmas has a habit of going wrong. In Bunyan's day, people were using it as an excuse to drink heavily and going round scaring each other. And looking into the future, there's all kinds of weird stuff like the Grinch, Frosty the Snowman and some abomination called Kris Kringle that's probably based on the word "Christ", but I can barely bring myself to look.'

'Maybe a Dickensian Christmas isn't so bad, after all,' said the author.

'Did you just make an adjective of your own surname?' said the angel.

'I did.'

'Too soon.'

'Reckon?'

'Reckon. Goodnight, Mr Dickens.'

CR&O

Ascension 2 – not quite The Return

There are some things about Jesus and the gospel that are so obvious and so big that it's hard to step back far enough to see them. Here's one. Isn't it odd that Jesus, God Incarnate, could have started a megachurch, but didn't? He spoke to crowds, but they didn't exactly prove loyal when it came to Pilate offering them back their wonder-worker. Jesus' earthly ministry was short. But it was also small. Seventy were sent out to spread the word, but it's only a brief incident, and how many of those remained with Jesus? In John 6 we read that many disciples walked away when Jesus started saying hard things.

Jesus worked with a small group of 12 men, and a few women. But even one of those 12 was a wrong'un. And of that remaining 11, he seemed to be especially close to Peter, John and his brother James. It's so intimate.

How do the disciples respond? By vying with each other for position. It's pretty pathetic and sobering. At one point, James and John's mum gets involved and tries to bend Jesus to her will on the seating arrangements in heaven (Matthew 20). John's Gospel even ends with this kind of motif.

We'll have a look at that shortly, but let's go back to the Ascension in Luke that we considered and messed around with at the very beginning of the book and see how the power struggle continues.

[Jesus] led them out as far as Bethany, and he lifted up his hands, and blessed them. While he blessed them, he withdrew from them, and was carried up into heaven. They worshipped him.

Early manuscripts do not include the following
So Peter said, 'Okay, then. Time to return to Jerusalem with great joy. Come on, let's go.'

'Whoa, whoa, whoa,' said John. 'Who died, rose again and put you in charge?'

'No offence, Peter, but I'd always seen John as the natural next in line,' said another disciple.

'Seriously?' said Peter.

'Well, unaccustomed as I am to public speaking, I'm sure I could run things for a while. As long as everyone was cool with that?' said John.

'Why should you be in charge?' said Peter.

'I don't want to pull rank, but I'm John? The disciple whom Jesus loved?' said John.

'So you keep saying, but Jesus kind of loved everyone,' said Peter. 'If there's one thing we've learned in the last three years, it's that Jesus loves us.'

'You think I don't know that? He IS love,' said John. 'He just loved me the most.'

'Whoa!' said another disciple. 'Jesus did not have favourites. He loved everyone just the same. Especially the disciples. No special treatment or inner circle or . . . What?'

Peter and John looked at each other.

'That's not quite true,' said John. 'He loved both of us a lot.'

'Hands up who was invited by Jesus to go up the mountain for the transfiguration?' said Peter.

'Yeah, that was pretty amazing,' said John, putting up his hand. He permitted Peter to high-five it.

'The transfigur-whatnow?' said the other disciple. 'I didn't hear about that.'

'We met Moses and Elijah,' said John. 'You should have seen Peter. He was like, "Let me build you shelters."'

'Can we not go over that again?' said Peter.

'And the rest of us were sitting around at the bottom of the mountain with no idea this was all going on,' said the other disciple. 'Unbelievable. You think you know someone.'

'Look, erm, nameless disciple,' said John.

'Thaddeus!' said Thaddeus. 'How many times do I have to tell you?! If you're gonna be in charge, you could at least remember my name!'

'Don't worry, Thaddeus,' said Peter. 'John's not going to be in charge. I am.'

'Sorry, but why would Jesus put you in charge?' said John. 'You're a fisherman. No offence.'

'None taken,' said Peter. 'A fisherman's a good guy to have around in a crisis.'

'Except in the last crisis, when Jesus was being crucified,' said Thaddeus. 'You denied him three times!'

'Thank you so much for bringing that up,' said Peter.

'Cock-a-doodle-doo!' said Thaddeus.

'Ooh, too soon, Thaddeus,' said John. 'Waaay too soon.'

And then Peter said, 'Jesus and I had a private conversation.'

At that moment, a heavenly host appeared. And John was quite surprised.

Peter said, 'Jesus said, "You are Peter, and on this rock I will build my church, and the gates of hell will not overcome it. I will give you the keys of the kingdom of heaven; whatever you bind on earth will be bound in heaven, and whatever you loose on earth will be loosed in heaven." See, John? On me. "Peter." This rock. Me. See what he's done there? Petros means "Rock". What's got two thumbs and is called Peter? This guy!'

Peter pointed at himself using only his thumbs.

Then Thaddeus said, 'I thought your name was Simon.'

'Shut up,' said Peter. 'It is. Was. But it must be for this reason Jesus decided to call me Peter.'

'Didn't he call you "Satan" at one point?' said Nathanael.

'Don't you start,' said Peter.

'Oh, yes,' said Thaddeus. 'I remember. "Get behind me, Satan!"'

'So what if he did?' said Peter.

'You don't want Satan running the church, do you?' said Thaddeus.

'Well, I've been given the keys,' said Peter.

'And what happens when you die? Who gets them then?' said John.

'Not you,' said Peter.

'I didn't mean it like that,' said John. 'I just worry that a successor to Peter might start to get a bit carried away with their power and authority. Over time.'

'Good point,' said Thaddeus. 'Give it, say, fifteen hundred years and there's a chance this "head of the church" person could react badly to criticism and be slow to bring in reforms.'

'Possibly leading to a schism,' said Nathanael.

'Nah,' said Peter. 'Can't see that happening. It'll be fine. Anyway, shall we "return to Jerusalem with great joy"?'

'Fine,' said Thaddeus.

'Suppose so,' said Nathanael.

'You're the boss,' said John. 'Apparently.'

This is not the word of the Lord.
Thanks be to God.

CRSO

The final chapter

Having kids has undoubtedly changed me. I've learned an awful lot about my relationship with God through how my kids relate to me. When they doubt my word, when they distrust my promises, when they react against my good intentions and consistently underestimate my enormous love for them, I remember that this is how I am with God.

One of the pleasures of parenthood for me, at least, is reading to my kids at bedtime. Even though they are now 12 and 10 at the time of writing, I still do it. It was through reading *The Chronicles of Narnia* to my children that I really appreciated how truly brilliant these books are. As a child, I found reading to be a chore, and no one read these stories to me. The BBC TV adaptations were okay, but a little stilted, and, let's face it, the telly never truly captures a book but becomes its own thing.[1]

Another favourite I never tire of reading to my kids is *Winnie-the-Pooh*. When they were small, they loved them as stories, but can now hear them differently, as I heard them when I was a teenager. Yes, I listened to them as a teen. Being the youngest of four, with three busy older sisters, I spent a lot

---

1 I remember a review of the TV adaptations of the *Sharpe* novels, by Bernard Cornwell. The critic quoted *Forsyte Saga* director James Cellan Jones who said, 'Second-rate novels often make first-rate television,' which is rather a backhanded compliment. I can't find the original review but James Cellan Jones is quoted in Peter Fiddick, 'James Cellan Jones obituary', *The Guardian*, 10 October 2019, <https://theguardian.com/tv-and-radio/2019/oct/10/james-cellan-jones-obituary> (accessed 29 January 2021).

of time on my own (quite happily). I would cheerfully listen to the spoken word for hours on end.

We had two audio cassettes of *The House at Pooh Corner* being read by Lionel Jeffries, who is, for me, the definitive reader of the stories, not least because he does Tigger properly – as an Indian. After all, where do tigers come from? Anyway, I loved them as a teenager and listened to them on a regular loop, along with some audio captures on a cassette player of some episodes of *Blackadder*.[2]

As I read, often with the same intonations and, yes, accents as Lionel Jeffries, my children can hear all the irony, subtext and callbacks that are laced through A. A. Milne's classic tales. (And I've also been showing them selected episodes of *Blackadder*.)

But I have changed again. I am now a parent. Therefore, I want to sob when I read the ending when we leave them in an Enchanted Place. Christopher Robin is growing up and will be going away. Pooh, his favourite, doesn't quite understand. Childhood is drawing to a close, as it will soon for my own children. The ending is beautiful, emotional and wistful.

This is the feeling I get when I read the final chapter of John's Gospel, in which Jesus is so intimate and tender with his disciples, especially Peter and John. Jesus is on the shore and calls the seven disciples listed, 'Children'. He then causes a miraculous catch of fish, but when Peter, astonished to see his Lord, dives into the water to swim to him, he sees that somehow Jesus already has fish.

At that moment, Jesus doesn't wag his finger at Peter for his

---

2 Which is why I can recite pretty much verbatim the Dr Johnson and Duke of Wellington episodes of *Blackadder the Third*. By the time *Blackadder Goes Forth* came out, we had a Panasonic video recorder. Joy of joys!

three denials or give him a divine 'I told you so'. Jesus tenderly offers him reconciliation.

Spoiling it

This verse, however, is preceded by this unseemly jealousy from Peter, who is having a private one-to-one with Jesus when 'the disciple whom Jesus loved' turns out to be following them. Peter wants to know more about what will become of this disciple, whom we traditionally take to be John.[3] There is clearly a bit of rivalry going on here. And Jesus' reply is surprising and pointed: 'If I desire that he stay until I come, what is that to you? You follow me.'[4] And then the disciples all draw the wrong conclusion and spread it around.

This disciple, whom Jesus loved, explains that he is the one bearing witness to what he has seen, and then we come to the final verse of the final chapter, which feels like it's straight out of A. A. Milne to me:

Now there are also many other things that Jesus did. Were every one of them to be written, I suppose that the world itself could not contain the books that would be written.
(John 21.25, ESV)

---

3 There's a fine biblical scholar called Richard Bauckham who contends that the author of John's Gospel is not John the apostle, son of Zebedee and one of the twelve. But there is another John, 'disciple whom Jesus loved', John the Elder. Neither is to be confused with John the Baptist. But it's probably a bit late to be getting into that. See Richard Bauckham, *Jesus and the Eyewitnesses: The Gospels as eyewitness testimony*, 2nd Edition (Grand Rapids: Eerdmans, 2017).

4 I love this verse. In fact, *What Is That To You?: The overlooked Christian discipline of minding your own business* is the front runner as the title for my next book.

The sequel

But it's not over. There is a sequel. And like most sequels to things you love, you realize when you have it that it's not quite what you wanted. From John we get the book of Revelation. It's the tricky second album, which puzzles and baffles even the most hardcore fans. Moreover, learned brothers and sisters who are of one mind on so many other things interpret these words radically differently.[5]

But why is this revelation to John? Peter is the Rock on whom the church is built, to whom the keys are given. Peter is the first Bishop of Rome and essentially the founder of the church. And yet this special revelation is given to John, rather than Peter.

And then I wondered if the angels who visited John had actually visited Peter first and, given his track record in the Gospels as the Homer Simpson of the piece, it didn't go quite as was hoped. Therefore, I present to you the previously deleted Apocalypse of Peter. And so:

A very early discarded manuscript says the following
The Revelation of Jesus Christ, which God gave him to show to his servants the things that must soon take place. He made it known by sending his angel to his servant, Peter.

I, Peter, your brother and partner in the tribulation and the kingdom, was in bed when I heard a loud

---

5 To prove this point, there are two recent commentaries on Revelation by Ian Paul and Peter Leithart, both of whom I have the blessing of knowing a bit. They are both fine, intelligent and godly men with whom I agree on almost everything. And yet they see the book of Revelation completely differently and each interpretation mostly excludes the other's.

trumpet sound. Which happens a lot when I'm in bed, but this was a different kind of trumpet sound.

It was like a trumpet saying, 'Write down what you see in a book and send it to the seven churches.'

And I said, 'What, like a round robin?'

And the voice said, 'Yes, I suppose so. Now write this down.'

Then I turned to the voice that was speaking to me, and I looked and I saw one like a son of man, clothed with a robe, with white hair, eyes aflame and feet like bronze, and his voice was like rushing waters. And I said, 'Ooh, rough night?' And out of his mouth came a sharp two-edged sword, and that was pretty freaky and I was starting to think that cheese before bedtime was a mistake.

And I looked and he shone like the sun shining in full strength, and I fell face down, and he said, 'I died and behold I am alive forevermore. I have the keys of Death and Hades. Therefore write down the things you have seen . . . Why aren't you writing this down?'

And then I looked and I couldn't find my pen. Anywhere.

And I saw something like a pen. But it was just a stick. And not a pen.

And then I found a pencil and then I saw a scroll and began to write, but then an angel said, 'Actually, that's my scroll. Get your own from that angel over there.'

And another angel gave me a little scroll and told me to eat it. And I asked if this would make me really small or really big, and he just shook his head as if he knew I'd say something like that.

And I began to weep as it was all going wrong, and I imagined John, the disciple whom Jesus loved, having a good old laugh at my expense.

'Weep no more,' said the angel. 'Behold, see what I am showing you.'

And I saw a woman on a red dragon rising from the sea and a war in heaven between Michael and his angels, fighting, and there was a serpent bound for a thousand years and there was a period of great tribulation, and I saw one like the Son of Man returning to reign for a thousand years.

And I called out to the angel, 'Can I just stop you there?'

'What?' said the angel, pinching his nose in stress, and then a sword came out of it.

And I said, 'That's just showing off.'

And the angel said, 'You asked me to stop the show. What is it?'

And I said, 'About this period of a thousand years. How exactly does that work?'

And the angel said, 'What does it matter? It's all metaphorical.'

'Is it, though?' I said. 'I've just got a feeling that this is something that Christians will really obsess over at some point in the next two thousand years. How does the order go? We should nail this whole "thousand years" thing down.'

And the angel said, 'Look, just keep watching, will you?'

And then I looked and I saw people from every nation, gathered together in strange clothes and walking slowly in a giant circle.

And the angel said, 'Sorry, that's the opening ceremony from the Montreal Olympics. That's the wrong tape. You made me lose my place. Bear with.'

And then I saw a city and a river and a tree and a lamb, and then the visions and dreams were no more. And I woke up.

My pillow was on the other side of the room for some reason, and I had a really dry mouth. And I checked, and there was no sword in there.

And I looked and I saw on the bedside table a small scroll. And I opened it and it said, 'Thanks, Peter. No offence, but I think I'll try John for this, if it's all the same to you. Yours, the angel.'

This is not the word of the Lord.
Thanks be to God.

૨૭ ૪૦

Epilogue – *Pilgrim's Progress* Part 3

Weary from his travels, Christian was now on the Enchanted Ground. The air was sweet and the birds sang. Safely beyond the Valley of the Shadow of Death and out of the reach of Giant Despair, Christian was surprised to encounter a man sitting at a desk, scribbling on paper.

'Hello,' said Christian. 'What are you writing?'

'I'm rewriting,' said the man at the desk, whose name was Sitcom Writer. 'I was given notes.'

'It is good to seek excellence,' said Christian. 'What are you working on? Is it something that lifts the soul and glorifies our Lord and Saviour?'

'It's a sitcom script,' said Sitcom Writer. 'For that is my lot in life. To amuse and entertain.'

'Oh,' said Christian. 'Anything I might have seen?'

'People often ask that,' said Sitcom Writer. 'But since you're the product of a Puritan who would probably ban theatre, I doubt it.'

'The theatre pays court to the affections that plunge the soul ever deeper into corruption.'

'And yet this tale of *Pilgrim's Progress* is regularly adapted by Christian theatre companies,' said Sitcom Writer. 'That's funny.'

'I fail to see the humour in it.'

'I thought you might,' said Sitcom Writer. 'Which is also funny.'

'I suppose you think you're funny,' said Christian.

'I am funny,' said Sitcom Writer. 'I'm a sitcom writer. My livelihood depends on it. But I'm not sure I could ever use my gifts in a way that would satisfy a serious man like you.'

'Following Christ is an undertaking of the utmost gravity,' said Christian. 'I'm sure comedy has its place, but I'd rather be a serious man rejoicing with the saints in heaven than a laughing man in the fires of hell.'

'I think you misunderstand joy, heaven and laughter,' said Sitcom Writer.

'Those who laughed at Jesus put him to death,' said Christian.

'They didn't laugh. They sneered. And only after they had nailed him to a cross,' said Sitcom Writer. 'Anyone reading the Gospels would see that the men who executed our Lord and Saviour Jesus Christ were serious men.'

'You call me a Pharisee or Sadducee?' said Christian.

'I do not. Your faith is sincere and your Christian journey a blessing to many throughout the centuries,' said Sitcom Writer. 'Maybe this is as much to do with temperament as godliness.'

'That may be,' said Christian. 'Perhaps things seem very different in your era. In mine, people go to prison for saying things they are not allowed to say.'

'It's getting that way in mine, actually,' said Sitcom Writer. 'I don't know if you read *The Sacred Art of Joking*, but . . .'

'Prison can be a blessing,' interrupted Christian. 'It was while in prison that my author began to write this allegory,' said Christian.

Sitcom Writer was about to say that it wasn't an allegory, but decided to leave it.

'Your author is a true inspiration to me,' said Sitcom Writer. 'He was prepared to speak the truth plainly. And suffer the consequences. I pray I will always do that.'

'And I will pray for you most earnestly,' said Christian. 'Now why don't you join me on my journey?'

'I will,' exclaimed Sitcom Writer, throwing down his quill. 'That way, I won't have to think of an ending to my script. Endings are always the hardest bit.'

'Ah, very clever,' said Christian. 'Do you see what he's done there, readers?'

Sitcom Writer stood amazed. Christian winked.

Christian said, 'On my travels, I met a man called Breaking the Fourth Wall.'

'I know,' said Sitcom Writer, increasingly puzzled. 'I wrote that bit. What's going on?'

'Words are powerful. They take on a life of their own,' said Christian. 'I reflected on Breaking the Fourth Wall and realized that John the Evangelist does this in his Gospel. And so does our Lord himself when he was born into the very world that he spoke into being.'

'Wow. Good point,' said Sitcom Writer. 'I don't really know what to do with that.'

'Me neither,' said Christian. 'But we have eternity to reflect. Shall we?'

Christian and Sitcom Writer walked on to the Celestial City.

CR℘

WE HAVE A VISION OF A WORLD IN WHICH EVERYONE IS TRANSFORMED BY CHRISTIAN KNOWLEDGE

As well as being an award-winning publisher, SPCK is the oldest Anglican mission agency in the world.

Our mission is to lead the way in creating books and resources that help everyone to make sense of faith.

Will you partner with us to put good books into the hands of prisoners, great assemblies in front of schoolchildren and reach out to people who have not yet been touched by the Christian faith?

To donate, please visit www.spckpublishing.co.uk/donate or call our friendly fundraising team on 020 7592 3900.

An easy way to get to know the Bible

'For those who've been putting aside two years in later life to read the Bible from cover to cover, the good news is: the most important bits are here.' Jeremy Vine, BBC Radio 2

The Bible is full of dramatic stories that have made it the world's bestselling book. But whoever has time to read it all from cover to cover? Now here's a way of getting to know the Bible without having to read every chapter and verse.

No summary, no paraphrase, no commentary: just the Bible's own story in the Bible's own words.

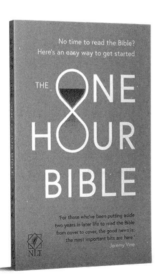

'What an amazing concept! This compelling, concise, slimmed-down Scripture is a must for anyone who finds those sixty-six books a tad daunting.'
Paul Kerensa, comedian and script writer

'A great introduction to the main stories in the Bible and it helps you to see how they fit together. It would be great to give as a gift.'
Five-star review on Amazon

The One Hour Bible
978 0 281 07964 3 • £4.99